COSMIC HARMONY
A Spiritual Roadmap to Personal Transformation and Abundance

This book is dedicated to those special individuals, both past and present, who helped me find my way.

To my sister-in-law **Judy**, who possessed the wisdom to steer me right; and to **John D.,** who taught me how to have a conversation, to be grateful and demonstrated what it truly means to care for oneself.

To **George H. ("Tree Farm George")**, whose thoughtful words are echoed within these pages, and to **Wayne W.,** the gentlest human being I have ever known and for his unwavering presence.

To **Linda G.,** who helped me recognize and change my most destructive thought patterns.

And finally, to my seven wonderful **siblings**, whose immense strength, support, and love have been my greatest fortune.

Table of Contents

Preface

Like many people, I spent years living out of a **conditioned mind,** unaware that my thoughts were the true cause of my experience. I was caught in a cycle of heedless action and careless living, constantly fighting people, places and all that is the outer world and its circumstances, never realizing that my own thinking was the cause of all my conflicts.

I vividly remember realizing this futility during a moment of profound personal crisis: I had finally exhausted every resource, hit a wall of defeat, and understood that I could not win the battle alone. I had to admit defeat and accept help. It was an act of Grace that led me to a peaceful path where wise teachers taught me a radical truth: The only way to change my life was to change my own thinking.

This journey of transformation, rooted in timeless **spiritual guidelines** and structured principles, led me not only to freedom but to a world of knowledge I never knew existed. My continued spiritual searching led me to discover the profound truths within **Hermetic principles and New Thought ideas.** My conviction grew: these teachings and the spiritual roadmap that saved my life and gave a whole new meaning to living are **universal.** They can help anyone organize their consciousness and improve their life.

That is the very reason I have composed this book. I have integrated these life-changing principles—from the practical wisdom that guided my own sobriety and happiness to the philosophical insights of conscious creation—into a single volume. This book provides a roadmap from a conditioned mind to an awakened one.

My hope is that it will guide you to a life of peace, purpose, and lasting joy. Your thoughts are the true architects of your reality, and you will always get out of life what you put into it. As we begin, know this: **the power you crave has been within you all along. And you are greater than you know.**

The wisdom contained in these pages is not a theory, but a blueprint for alignment with **Universal Law.** By mastering your inner architect, you will secure the ultimate reward: a life defined by **Absolute Freedom and Peaceful Harmony** within the cosmos.

Introduction

Life is a gift; enjoy the unwrapping of your experiences!

My mother always said, "Save the bow," while someone was opening a present. Unwrapping your life is similar. The bow on top is your breath, a simple reminder to be thankful for each moment. This life is an unconditional gift, nothing is required of you to have it. All you need to do is accept it with joy and gratitude.

Note: For the purpose of this book, we refer to concepts that exist primarily in spiritual, metaphysical, and social contexts, not as a formal law of nature like gravity or electromagnetism.

"The lips of wisdom are closed except to the ears of understanding." — The Kybalion

The fact you are reading this book tells me you **ARE** ready for it. Be sure to keep an open mind, this is crucial to your progress.

The Problem: Preconditioned Thinking

Naturally, developing conscious awareness while growing spiritually is a gradual process. But this journey is often blocked by the weight of a conditioned mind. We are all inherently preconditioned even before birth— beliefs, superstitions, old ideas, and thought processes get passed down through generations.

This leads to thinking that is narrow and resistive and often filled with mistrust and doubt. Too many people allow self-defeating negative thoughts and unreasonable fabricated fears to dictate their lives. Freedom, harmony, and joy remain elusive because many are unaware that their thinking is the true cause of their experience, let alone that there is a way to take command of it. Even the most basic exchange, communication, becomes complicated and tricky when two conditioned minds attempt to connect.

The Roadmap: Spiritual Principles and Conscious Awareness

The good news is that this ignorance and disillusionment are avoidable. The key to transformation lies in the development of conscious awareness. Development comes from right knowledge, and the recognition and acceptance of truth.

This book provides the necessary **roadmap**. It is the result of a personal spiritual journey that led me to integrate fundamental spiritual principles, Ancient philosophy, the profound truths within the seven Hermetic laws, and New Thought ideas. My conviction grew: these teachings and spiritual guidelines are universal and can help anyone organize their consciousness and improve their life.

The importance of gaining this knowledge of spiritual principles and universal laws cannot be understated. Although you'll find definite suggestions for practical application, this book is primarily structured as a philosophical "what's what" as opposed to 'how to. We take a deep dive into the unchanging universal principles and the mechanics of self-awareness. The material is arranged in a **logical and progressive** sequence for best practice, ensuring that by focusing on this foundational knowledge, you gain the tools necessary for your **transformation**.

Action and Freedom

The process of awakening requires willingness, courage, and integrity. It means letting go of old ideas, rising above personal obstacles, and embracing humility and forgiveness.

Your external world is the mirror that reflects your thoughts *(whether you are aware of them or not)*. Since mind is creative, you attract what you feel and create what you can imagine. Therefore, you must pay strict attention to what you think, say, and do.

At first, keep it simple: get acquainted with your breathing and five senses. The important thing is that you must learn by doing. Effects are your only gauge as to whether your thinking is constructive and aligned properly.

Rest assured, you are never alone in this life. Consider this book your invitation to the transformative knowledge and necessary action required to begin living consciously. Lasting joy and perfect harmony are already yours if you want them.

The Progressive Chain of Conscious Living:

Spiritual/Internal: Mental and spiritual progress leads to improved circumstances and environment.

Foundation/Knowledge: Knowledge leads to growth.

Activation: Inspiration leads to action.

Result/External: Perception leads to opportunity.

The ultimate destination of this spiritual roadmap is not merely external success or improved health; it is the **recognition of your true, infinite nature**. The greatest spiritual teachers and philosophers across millennia—from the ancient wisdom of **Advaita Vedanta** to modern New Thought—confirm this one unifying truth: **You are the same in kind and quality as the Universal Energy.** The difference is only one of degree.

To use a simple analogy: Your consciousness is a **drop of ocean** water that is still, in every way—its composition, its essence, its quality—identical to the **whole ocean**. You are not separated from the source of all power; you are that power in miniature. As Charles F. Haanel summarizes in The Master Key System: **"The principle which enables you to think... is the Infinite Mind of the Universe."** This realization is the absolute foundation of **Self-Mastery**. Once you accept that you are one with the **Universal Mind**, the only thing separating you from limitless power is the conditioned thinking of your mind.

I Conscious Mind

Consciousness is the nature of reality aware of itself.

Figure 1.1

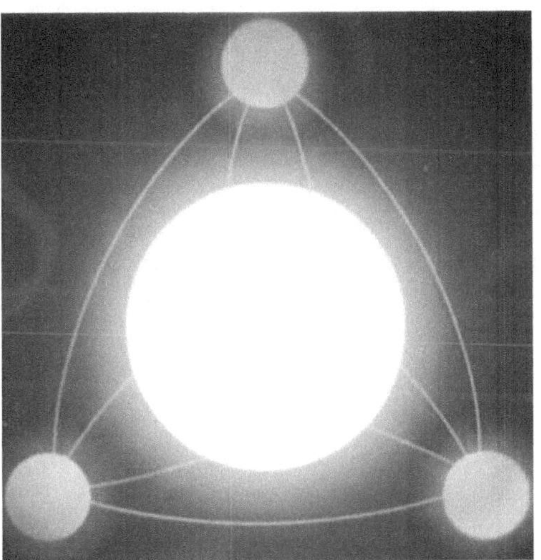

Figure 1.1 This illustrates the three key components of your being: the small upper sphere (often depicted in blue) represents the **Mind**, the lower left sphere (amber) represents the **Body**, and the lower right sphere (teal) represents the **Spirit**. The large, glowing white central sphere is **Consciousness**—your true self—which contains and encompasses all three.

For the human experience, the most basic, irreducible fact is **not the thought itself,** but the **awareness of the thought.** While Descartes asserted, **"I think therefore I am,"** this book elevates that fundamental idea: "I am aware therefore I am." This is to say that **YOU** are pure consciousness, the 'container' of reality which also contains your perceptions, emotions, and thoughts. This pure consciousness is the spiritual 'I,' limitless, ever present, and unbound by the physical body or temporary personality. We will most certainly delve into this bold idea ahead in Chapter III, in the section titled The **Spiritual Conduit,** where we talk about your true nature.

Our ability to think, to even exist, is founded on a fundamental 'What Is'— a perfectly balanced system of Universal Laws that govern all creation. This system unites consciousness and Spiritual Energy as one and the same. More on this profound concept further in Chapter XI.

The purpose of this book is to present the **'What Is,'** of life, focusing on the reality of Universal Laws, the power of ancient philosophy, and the practical application of Spiritual Principles. We do not question why reality is structured this way; **we accept that it is**. We are only concerned with **'what' and how it works,'** for the answers to these questions are the true key to mastery; asking why is an inquiry into futility. We are ultimately seeking knowledge of 'what is' and how to exist within 'what is' as a unified field of energy. Therefore, we approach personal development as a journey of the parts (your mind and body) realizing their identity with the whole, (a unified field of spiritual energy) and learning the impersonal rules (Universal Laws and energetic reciprocity) that govern their interaction.

Many people feel that life just happens to them, leading to mistaking routine for destiny. But there is a state of Cosmic Harmony where your inner life resonates perfectly with the universal flow. This book offers a clear roadmap for awakening to that conscious existence. I will tell it to you plainly: the profound shift presented here requires more than casual reading—it demands your genuine commitment and study. So before we go on, I invite you to weigh the reward and answer this question: Do you desire **Absolute Freedom**—the liberation from fear and the confines of old ideas? Do you wish to be the master of yourself and learn the power to change your destiny —enough to commit to radically changing the way you think and live?

Your acceptance and desire for true understanding are the foundation for the essential work: uniting the personal, objective mind with the impersonal, Inner Mind (subconscious) within you. This integration is the key to unlocking your true self, claiming your mastery, and finally participating in the complete harmony of the cosmos. The path is clear, and the potential for liberation is boundless. **Welcome to the beginning of your conscious creation.**

An Introduction to the Thinking Mind and Its Limitations

Your world is not at the command of an invisible hand, but your own conscious one—or rather, the coordinated action of your inner minds. The journey to conscious living is one way to discover this personal authority and learning the spiritual principles that govern and guide your alignment with the **fundamental Spiritual Energy**. This core idea—that consciousness is the primary substance of reality—has been taught by mystics for millennia and is now finding powerful support in modern theoretical physics and philosophy.

The Core Principle: The Indispensable Premise

To achieve **Absolute Freedom**, you must first comprehend the foundational 'What Is' premise:

Consciousness is the **Primary Substance of Reality**, and all **Universal Laws** govern its interaction with **Spiritual Energy.** This understanding—that your individual awareness is one with the Universal Source—is the indispensable premise for all the disciplines that follow.

The first key to conscious living is the realization that your circumstances are simply the inner mind being reflected. This understanding is the foundation of all right thinking. Acceptance of this basic truth is your green light for moving forward.

The Absolute Reward: Why Discipline Matters

You may wonder why this work, which include **Conscious Awareness Disciplines,** is worth the effort, especially when escaping into vice or simple comfort seems easier. But this comfort is a profound illusion. The true motivation for awakening is found in the immediate reward of **Absolute Freedom.** The ultimate payoff for doing this work is this:

Freedom from Reaction: You gain the ability to choose your response to life, instantly ceasing to be a victim of your environment, your past, or the conditioned thinking of others.

Unbreakable Hope: Your hope and motivation become unbreakable because they are internally sourced—they are no longer reliant on external circumstances, people, or possessions.

End of Separation: You achieve genuine, permanent connection, dissolving the mental barriers that cause feelings of loneliness and isolation.

The real work isn't uncomfortable; the alternative—being perpetually driven by fear—is. You are choosing the profound ease of Self-Mastery over the perpetual struggle of oblivion.

A wise old friend told me, "If you put comfort first, you lose." It was perfect motivation for me to learn how to be master of my own thinking.

🔑 Foundational Terms

Before we explore the limitations of the thinking mind, let's establish the foundational terms that describe your inner world. These concepts are the tools you'll use to distinguish between what is real and what is merely perceived.

A. The Fundamental Capacity: **Awareness**

Term	Definition	Connection to Growth
Awareness	The raw, fundamental capacity to perceive. It is the non-judgmental "light" of your consciousness, a basic state of being awake and sensing.	It is the starting point for all spiritual development. You can be aware of the **outer world** (sensory data) or the **inner world** (thoughts, feelings).
Conscious Awareness	A term we use frequently in this book, emphasizing the **intentional and disciplined application** of your fundamental awareness.	Simply being conscious is passive; achieving **conscious awareness** is the active step toward self-mastery and controlling your mental narrative.

B. The Mechanics of Attention: **Noticing & Mindfulness**

The Conscious Mind uses the capacity of Awareness through specific actions:

Noticing Thoughts: This is a specific, deliberate action. It's the process of turning your awareness inward to observe a thought, feeling, or sensation as a separate object in your mind, rather than being identified with it. This action immediately establishes a necessary distance between "you" (the observer) and the thought (the observed).

Mindfulness: This is the formal practice or the "how-to" method. It's the disciplined act of intentionally bringing your awareness to your present experience—including thoughts, feelings, and sensations—without judgment. Mindfulness is the training ground for your intellect, strengthening your ability to manage the mental processes that feed the subconscious mind.

C. The Dual Components of Mind

To understand how our inner world functions and how we achieve **cosmic harmony,** it is essential to keep the objective and subjective nature of the mind clear from the start.

Objective Mind (Conscious Mind): This is the **Thinking Mind** you are exploring in this chapter. It is the seat of reason, will, and discrimination. Its primary function is to be the guard that selects the information and commands passed to the Subconscious Mind.

Subjective Mind (Subconscious Mind): This is the **Hidden Mind** you will explore in Chapter II. It is non-selective, impersonal, and creative. This mind is the channel through which you coordinate the finite (your thoughts) with the infinite (Universal Power).

1. Sensory Awareness

The conscious mind begins its work by taking in raw data from the outer world. Your five senses—sight, sound, smell, taste, and touch—are the essential instruments through which consciousness processes this external information and the world of appearances. The ability to sense and perceive is what fundamentally shapes your upbringing, society, and immediate environment.

However, to assume your senses provide a complete or accurate appraisal of the world is a mistake. The physical world is filled with **illusions** that expose the limitations of our sensory tools. For instance, consider the temperature paradox: if you were to place one hand in hot water and the other in very cold water for a minute, and then immediately place both hands into a third bowl of lukewarm water, your hands would report contradictory data. One hand would feel the water is cold, and the other would feel it is hot. This momentary disorientation illustrates that our senses provide a **perspective only**, not the final truth, and can only be relied upon to a degree.

Still, the senses are indeed a way to navigate our human experience, and they evoke powerful, subjective joys—from the feeling of the sun's warmth to the delightful sound of a robin's song. For a long time, I took my own senses for granted; I would look but not truly see, hear but not really listen, and feel but not be aware of my feelings. While sensory data is essential, **it is limited, giving us an incomplete picture of the whole truth.** Our task, therefore, is to move beyond mere **sensory perception** and begin to understand the world we are perceiving.

One afternoon, while walking in the city, I encountered a destitute man who looked up at me and asked, "What's it all about?" This question, which has puzzled humanity for ages, left me momentarily speechless. For the first fifty years of my life, I had assumed it was unanswerable.

The man, without a doubt, perceived a physical world—the **Realm of Effect.** This is the world of results: the job you have, the money in your bank account, the relationships you maintain, and the body you inhabit. This realm is the visible, tangible consequence of forces that lie beneath the surface. His question, however, was the very essence of a thinking mind. While science provides a mountain of evidence about the physical world, it only details the "what" of existence. A thinking mind moves beyond the physical senses to seek the "why"—the deeper cause behind all the perceived effects.

Your conscious mind is the gateway through which you interact with this constant flow of phenomena. The Realm of Effect is the constantly changing landscape of people, places, and things that your physical senses gather and process. Crucially, your inner life—your thoughts, feelings, and beliefs—is the **Realm of Cause.** These inner decisions, often subconscious, dictate the circumstances that eventually materialize as effects in the outer world. The inquiry of the thinking mind, therefore, begins with the basic premise: **if I control the inner cause, I change the outer effect.**

However, as our brief exploration into sensory awareness revealed, this viewpoint is inherently limited. The answer to life's ultimate questions lies not in the material world, but in the depths of your own being. It's about recognizing your spiritual nature and consciously attending to your state of mind. This then is the inner world, a universe of causality as vast as the world without.

To begin, ask yourself what is profoundly important to you. What genuinely interests you and fuels your enthusiasm? You possess an inherent power to **choose your thoughts** and, by extension, the focus of your attention. This personal authority is the starting point for answering the ultimate question: what's it all about? **By consciously choosing the quality and nature of your inner thoughts and feelings—the Realm of Cause— you directly influence the outcomes you experience in the outer world.** At that point, you will come to understand, if only for yourself, what it is all about. And that, my friend, is a very satisfying feeling.

Conscious Awareness Discipline – **Stage One: Physical Stillness**

The journey inward begins with **mastering the body's movements.** Establishing conscious control over your physical form is the **essential prerequisite** for developing discipline over the restless nature of the mind.

1. Assume an upright posture, relaxed but never slouching and your feet flat on the floor.

2. For the next 15 to 30 minutes, actively commit to absolute stillness.

3. The core of this practice is to remain acutely aware of your body, intercepting the impulse to move before the movement occurs. Hold your body still but not stiff or tense..

4. Continue practicing until you can maintain perfect stillness for the designated duration.

3. The Nature of the Thinking Mind

a) **The Hard Problem of Consciousness**

While science can map the intricate workings of the brain and observe the physical processes that accompany thoughts, it remains stumped by one of the greatest mysteries of all: the "hard problem" of consciousness, a phrase coined by the philosopher David Chalmers. He distinguished between the "easy problems"—the functional aspects of the brain we can explain through neuroscience—and the "hard problem" of subjective, inner experience.

It isn't just about figuring out how the brain works; it's also about understanding why all that physical, chemical, and electrical activity gives rise to the feeling of being "you" the inner feeling of your own awareness. For all its incredible advances, science has no explanation for the "movie" that plays in the mind. It can describe the movie projector and the film, but not the feeling of watching it. This is where your spiritual inquiry truly begins—by looking beyond the physical mechanics and recognizing that the simple fact of inner awareness points directly to the truth: you are a spiritual being witnessing the mind and body.

b) The Core of Instinct

Beneath the intricate layers of your thinking mind lies an even older, more fundamental form of intelligence: **instinct**. It is the primal form of intelligence that drives and conditions the mind. Often dismissed as a mere "gut feeling" or animalistic urge, instinct is, in truth, a sophisticated and ancient guidance system, honed over eons of evolution. It is so powerful that it can override conscious thought, and understanding these primal responses offers invaluable insights into your deepest needs and reactions.

Simply put, instincts are built-in, unlearned patterns of behavior that help you survive and thrive. Unlike thoughts, which are actively constructed, instincts arise spontaneously and powerfully. They are pre-programmed responses designed to keep you safe and guide you toward what is fundamentally good for you. So trusting your instincts is always a good idea.

Instincts manifest in various ways:

Survival Responses: The most obvious are those related to self-preservation—the "fight or flight" and "freeze" responses in the face of danger. They also urge you to seek warmth when you're cold and drive you to find food and water. These are not learned; they are the **preprogrammed** biology already coded into your being.

Social & Emotional Needs: Beyond basic survival, you also have deeply ingrained instincts for connection, belonging, and emotional safety.

The discomfort of isolation or the pull toward community often stems from these primal social instincts.

Intuitive "Knowing": Often, what you describe as "intuition" or a "gut feeling" is a rapid, subconscious processing of information that taps into your instinctive awareness. This innate intelligence may manifest differently from person to person—as a physical sensation, an immediate insight, or a quiet, persistent inner voice—but its message is always the same: a primal guide toward your truth.

Becoming aware of your instinctive self is not about surrendering to uncontrolled impulses, however. It is about intelligent engagement with a profound part of your being. By recognizing the core of your instinct, you begin to understand your automatic reactions and connect to your innate wisdom. Learning to listen to these subtle cues can help you make more authentic decisions and recognize your true needs. By acknowledging this primal guidance system, you move closer to an integrated, conscious way of living, further harmonizing with the cosmos. To truly guide this journey, however, you must first understand Memory, the dynamic link between your past and your power in the present.

c) Memory: The Present's Echo

Memory shapes the present and the subconscious. Memory is not a separate time but the present's echo, a dynamic process that continuously shapes your identity and understanding of the world. It serves as the very foundation upon which your sense of self is built, actively informing you in the timeless "now."

Far from being simple storage, memory is a rich tapestry of experiences that helps you recognize patterns and make conscious choices in your immediate reality. Your brain weaves a thread that connects all experiences, and a basic understanding of this process offers profound insight into your inner landscape. At its core, memory is how the brain takes in, holds, and finds information so it can be utilized again. What you pay attention to in the present moment is more likely to become a lasting memory. Conscious attention, therefore, is another key to conscious living.

Memories, particularly long-term ones, deeply influence your sense of self. By becoming aware of how you frame and revisit past experiences, you can consciously shape your inner narratives. So it is by simply observing your own memories surface and recede that you will begin to see the intricate dance of your mind, a key in developing conscious awareness of your inner cosmos.

Furthermore, the subconscious holds a vast storehouse of memories that influence your current behavior. This is why affirmations and visualization are used.

The idea is to consciously place positive memories and associations into the subconscious, creating new patterns and rewriting your internal code.

d) The Inner Compass and Emotional Ownership

For much of my childhood, my feelings were suppressed. My fear of feeling anything at all left me adrift and without any emotional compass, creating a specific and difficult pattern for my emotional expression.

As a result, I found myself limiting the outward expression of my emotions mostly to anger. Perhaps because that was the only emotion I had witnessed being expressed by my dad mostly. Any other feelings I had such as fear, sadness or grief, were kept hidden and expressed in secret. The home was an environment where open communication about emotions wasn't encouraged, leaving me with the false belief that certain feelings might not be normal. Though my home was a good one, it lacked the emotional transparency needed for me to fully understand and process what I felt, leaving a significant part of me to sort it all out by myself. I learned the hard way. You do not have to take that path if you begin developing your conscious awareness now.

i. The Physiology of Emotion

It took many years of therapy before I was comfortable feeling my feelings, and even longer before I learned to express them in a healthy way. I'm still learning, but the main thing is I now know my feelings are neither right nor wrong but are simply part of what make me a human being. You and I have every right to feel them.

To be sure, feelings are complex, instinctive states of mind that arise from thoughts and circumstances. While they are a mental reaction, they are intricately linked to a cascade of neurochemical activity in the brain. This includes the release of neurotransmitters and hormones, as well as complex processing in key regions like the amygdala, hippocampus, and prefrontal cortex. These automatic, subconscious responses contribute to our subjective experiences and physical reactions. By understanding this relationship, you can recognize that emotions are not random; they are often a direct result of your own thought patterns.

ii. Emotional Responsibility

Given that emotions are a physiological response to thoughts, everyone is responsible for their own emotions. This may be a tough pill to swallow. The temptation is to say, "they made me feel" or "you make me feel" rather than owning the feeling by saying, "I feel this way or that." It requires a conscious shift in thinking to be able to accept your own feelings. The point here is not to blame others for how you feel. I am not saying that others don't contribute to how you feel, of course they can.

But they are not responsible for how you feel. This is the point I wish to emphasize; that the responsibility for your emotional well-being rests with you alone.

The moment you choose to understand your emotions you take another step on the journey to conscious awareness. Instead of being controlled by past experiences, you gain the power to consciously observe and work with your emotional state and learn to assume responsibility for it.

Say the affirmation: You got this. Say it like a friend would tell you. You got this! This is one sure way to take responsibility and in doing so you build your self-confidence

4. Witnessing the River of Consciousness

The **conscious** mind is a selective tool, endowed with the power of **will** and the responsibility of **choice**, and it operates using the faculties of discrimination and reason. Think of your brain as a tool for a single key purpose: that of **focusing your attention.**

Developing your attention is as simple as paying attention to what you're doing. And the closer you observe yourself, the better you'll be able to discern which thoughts are constructive and deserve your focused attention.

There is no need to fight negative feelings. Simply acknowledge them without judgment. By using your **intellect** to observe your emotions, you can keep them in check and gain an accurate understanding of your inner world. A helpful reminder is to always keep the **"I" (Intellect) over the "E" (Emotions)**.

Positive thoughts, on the other hand, and the good feelings that accompany them, motivate you to act and persevere in the face of challenges and help you build resilience.

In essence, **thought is cause**. You create your own world; your experience reflects that. Lots more on this topic in Chapter V, The *Law of Cause and Effect*. For now though, just understand that it is important to be able to control your thinking, emotions, and actions. Because thoughts, *whether you are aware of them or not,* and good or bad can shape your reality and influence your emotions, behaviors, and choices. So embrace the role of **witness consciousness** and prepare for the most exhilarating view of your own creation.

"Appearances are only a shadow of past beliefs." — Neville Goddard

The pursuit of happiness often leads people into cycles of striving, believing that wealth, status, or validation will finally bring peace. Yet, the opposite is true. As Charles Haanel observed, 'Harmony and happiness are states of consciousness and do not depend upon the possession of things.' This foundational truth frees you from the tyranny of external conditions. Your effort, therefore, must be placed on aligning your mind, not accumulating material objects, **as the world would have you believe.**

Conscious Awareness Discipline Stage Two– Physical Relaxation

Find a stable and upright posture, feet flat on the floor. Begin by consciously noticing any tension in your forehead, face, lips, and jaw. On an exhale, soften and release it. Move to your neck and shoulders, feeling the weight drop away as you let this tension go. Finally, allow the muscles of your back and legs to become heavy and deeply relaxed. And relax any tension you notice in the abdominal area.

Maintain a slow, steady breath and simply rest in this state of deep physical calm for 15 to 30 minutes. The continuous practice is designed to help you gain conscious, moment-to-moment control over your body's relaxation response.

A Crucial Reminder: This is a discipline of Conscious AWARENESS.

True awareness dissolves the moment you fall asleep. Your goal is to remain profoundly present and alert. You are not simply resting; you are actively practicing the observation of your inner world. You will gradually become more familiar with what this observation entails. This is your personal journey inward, fostering your conscious awakening.

The Foundation: Stillness, Relaxation, and Alertness

Every session begins with this 'sweet spot'—a state of profound physical ease coupled with acute mental alertness. This unique, dual state is the key to coordinating your conscious and subconscious minds. Do not be discouraged; holding this relaxed-but-alert state requires dedicated practice. However, it is in this quiet, profound stillness that you will begin to recognize the connected oneness of your objective thought, subjective feeling (or 'gut feeling'), and how it is all connected to a greater spiritual power.

II Subconscious Mind

Hidden Mind, The Creative Power

In Chapter I, we established the Conscious Mind as the seat of reason, will, and discrimination—the guard at the gate that selects the seeds of thought. We learned that while the Conscious Mind interacts with the physical **Realm of Effect**, true power lies within the inner world, a universe of causality as vast as the world without. This inner world is governed by the Subconscious Mind, often referred to as the **Hidden Mind**. It is the non-selective engine of your experience; it does not reason or judge, it simply acts, creating conditions that align precisely with the thoughts and feelings it is given.

To understand the immense creative power we are discussing, we turn to the words of Charles Haanel, who masterfully summarized the central principle of all conscious creation:

"The subjective mind is amenable to control by the conscious mind. It is a vital principle, receiving orders and executing them. It does not matter whether these thoughts are right or wrong, true, or false, its action upon them is the same."

— Charles F. Haanel, The Master Key System

This quote is the central thesis of our journey into the Subconscious Mind. It clearly establishes two essential facts: **control** and **creation**. Your conscious mind is responsible for issuing the "orders," but it is your subconscious mind, the creative force, which does the actual work of execution. The Subconscious Mind is the channel through which you coordinate the finite, temporary thought forms you select with the infinite, universal power that manifests them into your physical reality.

The Physiological Basis for Conscious Control

To fully grasp how your inner world creates your outer reality, it helps you to understand the physical systems that execute your mental commands. Learning to use both of these "brains" together is how you fully access the power within.

1. Central Nervous System (CNS): The Seat of Will

The Central Nervous System (CNS), which includes the brain and spinal cord, serves as the physical mechanism of your Conscious Mind.

Role: The CNS is the voluntary command center. It handles all higher functions like reasoning, decision-making, and deliberate thought.

Self-Awareness Tip: When you are calmly choosing your focus, making a rational decision, or engaging in conscious disciplines, your CNS is actively in control.

2. Sympathetic Nervous System (SNS): The Engine

The Sympathetic Nervous System (SNS) is a division of your involuntary nervous system. It serves as the physiological expression of your Subconscious Mind's automatic, mental, and emotional programming.

Role: The SNS governs the powerful "fight-or-flight" response. It immediately executes involuntary reactions to stress, such as increasing your heart rate or adrenaline.

Location and Awareness: This system's primary bundle of nerves is concentrated in the Solar Plexus (located in the pit of your stomach/upper abdomen). When you feel intense fear, anxiety, or gut-level stress, the tension you feel in this region is the SNS activating its powerful, automatic response and warning system.

Coordination: Understanding this system gives you a physical checkpoint for self-awareness. When you feel tension in the Solar Plexus, you know the subconscious/SNS is running a program. Your mastery lies in using your CNS/Conscious Will to redirect that energy.

3. The Silent Servant of the Will

You have **dominion** over both the conscious and subconscious mind. The conscious mind is the master, and the subconscious is the **silent servant of the will.** Unlike the conscious mind, however, the subconscious is impersonal and non-selective. It only knows how to do what it is told; it cannot debate the conscious thought that it receives. That absolute, unquestioning obedience is, in itself, a somewhat humorous notion, and yet it is the greatest truth of your mental architecture.

With this knowledge, you are empowered to impress the subconscious by concentrating on any desire you wish to manifest. It is also important to note that your subconscious mind is always absorbing information. This is why it is so crucial to be aware of the thoughts and beliefs you dwell on. Think of the subconscious as the background operating system (OS) of your mind. This OS is the true engine of manifestation. It runs actions and reactions that happen without you consciously needing to think about them—from controlling your heartbeat, not forgetting that you must continually breath as well as other complex activities like driving a car, right down to the automatic preprogramming of your life. This is also where habits, both good and bad, reside. Understanding this allows you to change unwanted habits by creating new and positive patterns.

It is critical to understand that conditions, environment, and all experiences in life are a direct result of a habitual or **predominant mental attitude.**

Your primary job is not to worry about how things will happen, but simply to provide clear, positive direction and allow your Silent Servant to work. This distinction is vital. And again, as Haanel instructs, when you are **'plainly stating to the subconscious mind certain specific things to be accomplished, forces are set in operation that lead to the result desired.'** However, he wisely cautions us to remember that **'it is not necessary to outline the method by which the subconscious will produce the results you desire. The finite cannot inform the infinite.'** This means your conscious mind's job is limited to providing the 'what,' leaving the limitless 'how' to the power within.

By focusing on the spiritual/internal, you naturally initiate a change from within which inevitably affects a change without. From this internal shift, you learn from mistakes, grow, and mature in your thought processes, improving your overall understanding of the way things work. Your experience will, without doubt, inspire you to keep learning and growing. It will help you understand and act in more productive and useful ways, which naturally leads to an improved perception where you will perceive greater and greater opportunities to pursue and succeed. This chain confirms that the foundation of all desirable change lies in the cultivation of the Inner Mind, establishing the correct spiritual and mental state first.

The Scientific Foundation: Neuroplasticity

What you are learning here is not just philosophy; it is supported by modern neuroscience. The ability to change unwanted habits and create new patterns is called neuroplasticity, which is the brain's power to rewire itself throughout life. Every time you consciously choose a new thought or perform a constructive action, you are strengthening new neural pathways in your mind's operating system. The brain is quite remarkable.

Conversely, the repetition inherent in bad habits carves deep, efficient, and often destructive pathways that the subconscious follows automatically. Conscious awareness discipline, however, allows you to intentionally decommission those old pathways and construct new and improved ones. Is this not great news?

Conscious Awareness Discipline – The Flow

To experience an **illumined mind,** you must cultivate the **art of mental detachment**—observing thoughts without engagement or judgment. When a thought, worry, or stressor arises, resist the impulse to analyze or fight it; instead, gently surrender it to the flow of Universal Energy.

A beautiful method for this is the **"Leaves on a Stream"** technique:

Visualize the Scene: Close your eyes and vividly imagine a calm, steady river flowing directly in front of you. Sense the environment: the smooth current, the banks, the sound of the river gently flowing.

Observe the Flow: Imagine any number or size of leaves floating slowly by on the surface of the water.

Load the Leaf: As any mental object arises—a doubt, fear, resentment, or any distraction—gently package that thought (as a word or a quick image) and mentally place it directly onto a passing leaf.

Release and Return: Watch the leaf and its burden drift downstream until it disappears completely from view. Allow it to leave you. Immediately return your awareness to the gentle flow, ready for the next leaf.

This discipline teaches your conscious mind that thoughts are not commands; they are simply objects that can be observed and released.

4. Emotional Power and Universal Law

The power of this inner operating system is amplified because it taps into a deeper, **universal intelligence**. It functions as the primary conduit between your personal mind and being in **harmony with the cosmos**. Because this system is non-judgmental and literal, it accepts every program (thought, belief, emotion) you run, treating it as a directive, and then works tirelessly—using universal laws—to manifest its equivalent in your external world. This makes your current predominant mental attitude the most crucial command you can issue. And emotions are the potent energy fueling the system.

Redirecting Emotional Power

Since the subconscious is primarily driven by the raw energy of emotion, you possess the power to transmute that energy. When an intense negative emotion like anger or frustration arises, you do not have to suppress it, nor must you let it dictate a harmful outcome; there is another way.

Instead, you can consciously acknowledge the raw, powerful feeling, then immediately re-route it. This action is never spontaneous; it must be a **deliberate choice** informed by awareness, requiring the coordinated effort of your Will and Intellect (the very tools of the Conscious Mind). The process involves three key steps:

a) **Acknowledge and Isolate** (Intellect): You must first use your intellect to witness the negative emotion without judgment. Name the feeling (e.g., "This is anger," "This is fear") and separate the raw energy from the destructive thought that caused it. This act of noticing—of simply being aware of the feeling as it arises—is the single most difficult but important factor for success. For readers new to conscious awareness, this initial recognition requires a fierce commitment to paying attention and is where your practice truly begins. Acknowledge what you are and be honest with yourself about it.

b) **Command and Re-Purpose** (Will): Next, you must exercise your will to immediately shift your focus away from the negative thought and toward a constructive alternative. Though you won't be as efficient in the beginning, with practice you become more conscientious of what you are doing. It takes your full attention; and not only a willingness to change but a sincere desire to.

Now of the moment of choice, command the powerful energy to fuel intense focus on a goal or another task you wish to complete. Use the energy for good and embrace the positive change you experience. Then it becomes a simple matter of persevering. Everyone has this capability and all you need to do is use it. Applying willpower only requires a conscious and deliberate intention.

You are the engineer who decides where the power flows; your emotions can work in your favor or NOT. But to achieve a positive outcome, you only need to change the target to a positive one. And you never have to go down a road you have doubts about.

The hidden minds unwavering obedience means the subconscious translates your persistent mental imagery and emotional state into corresponding actions and circumstances. Learning to manage this literal, powerful inner OS is the first step in moving from being an accidental programmer of negative thoughts to becoming a deliberate architect of your desired reality. What are your intentions?

5. Programming the Inner Operating System

Now that you understand the background operating system of your mind, it's time to take control of the keyboard. To effectively influence this hidden mind and transform your reality, you must become a **deliberate and consistent programmer.**

The following are the **four pillars of conscious programming**—fundamental methods for consistently impressing constructive thoughts and ideas upon your subconscious:

Positive Affirmations: This is the practice of consciously writing new code in your mind. By consistently affirming the good, you starve the negative and empower your mind toward a more powerful outcome.

Journaling: This is a method for externalizing your inner world. By writing down your thoughts and feelings, you gain critical distance and a new perspective, making it easier to identify and debug negative thought patterns.

Visualization: Your imagination is a powerful blueprinting tool. Use vivid mental imagery to see and feel the success and happiness you desire, empowering your subconscious to work tirelessly toward that ideal.

Meditation: Meditation is the ultimate practice for quieting the noise of the conscious mind and directly accessing the subconscious. Just know that even the slightest increase in conscious awareness is a sign of spiritual growth—and that consistent progress is all that truly matters.

Using these methods helps you consciously and systematically build constructive thought patterns and new and improved ways of thinking.

III Empowered Mind

"Nowhere man, please listen.

You don't know what you're missing.

Nowhere man, the world is at your command."

— The Beatles, "Nowhere Man"

The transformation from the 'Nowhere Man'—the passive effect of circumstance—to the 'Empowered Mind' begins with one breathtaking realization: the power you seek is not outside you. It is fundamental to your being. The wisdom of every major spiritual tradition confirms this truth. As the Bible states: 'Know ye not that ye are the temple of God, and that the Spirit of God dwelleth in you?' (1 Corinthians 3:16-17). This ancient text reminds us that the vast Universal Energy you seek is not separate from you; it is literally housed within your own mental and physical architecture. This means, simply and profoundly, that we are one with the Source. To begin your journey of Self-Mastery, you must turn your gaze inward and consciously recognize the incredible spiritual architecture that makes up the thinking mind.

1. The Creative Nature of Belief

The foundational wisdom of this chapter—and indeed, much of this book—is best encapsulated by the teachings of Neville Goddard. His core philosophy states that: **"The world around you is not fixed; it reflects your inner state. What you hold as true within will inevitably manifest without."** In short, your faith precedes your reality.

This radical idea means that your **mental state** is your true force. It is the master control panel, the lens through which you perceive reality, and the engine that drives your actions. The state of your mind, the sum of your thoughts, feelings, perceptions, and beliefs at any given moment, is so fundamental that nothing else truly matters. This idea is supported by principles in psychology, philosophy, and neuroscience:

a) **Confirmation Bias**: Your beliefs act as a powerful magnet. You tend to seek out and remember information that confirms what you already believe. It's why the phrase "people hear what they want to hear" is 100% true.

b) **The Placebo/Nocebo Effect**: This is a perfect example of the mind's power over matter. Believing a treatment will work can lead to physiological changes. Conversely, believing something will harm you can also manifest negative physical effects. This powerful inner force perfectly demonstrates that the power lies within you, not in external circumstances.

c) **Your Mental State Dictates Action**: A mental state of motivation and determination propels you toward your goals, while a state of lethargy or discouragement leads to inaction. The self-fulfilling prophecy shows this in action: your beliefs about yourself are blueprints for your behavior. Believing you will fail can lead you to unconsciously sabotage your efforts, thereby "proving" your belief. Conversely, believing in your success fuels the consistent action needed to achieve it.

d. **The Power of an Open Mind: Your mental states are not fixed**. While they are constantly shifting, you possess the power to direct them toward a specific, deliberate purpose. This conscious direction of your mind, however, is impossible without one vital precondition: the open mind.

An **open mind** is the ability to hold and consider **opposing ideas simultaneously,** recognizing that your current perspective is not the ultimate, final truth. As an old friend once told me, **"As soon as someone says, 'I know,' you cannot teach them anything."** Letting go of that "Mr. Know-it-all" mindset was a significant and necessary step for my growth and my direct access to limitless possibilities. Knowing is not all it's cracked up to be. Seeking to understand is what we are after- that's it.

Only by letting go of **false pride** and embracing a state of **active humility** can you truly begin to master your mental faculties. When you adopt this openness, you realize you were never powerless; you are simply allowing your inner awareness to recognize and unlock your fundamental creative powers.

For anyone seeking to understand themselves and the world around them, an open mind is the most vital prerequisite. Beware of the ego's false certainty; the moment you conclude you have nothing left to learn, your growth ceases. Realizing your connection to 'what is' begins with this profound openness—a willingness to accept truths that may challenge your preconceived notions. By remaining open, you will find the Truth that is deep within you.

This principle is essential because, as a fundamental tenet of New Thought, we understand that substance takes form according to mental demand—meaning your inner world is the sole architect of your outer experience.

"Belief overrides circumstances." — Neville Goddard

2. Your Fundamental Powers

"Whether you think you can or think you can't, you are right. "Henry Ford

As Henry Ford understood, success is directly dependent on the thoughts you cultivate. The way you think about yourself, and the world is not a passive activity; it's a **fundamental power** you possess. By learning to direct your thoughts toward a specific end, you can create the life you want. The power of thought is a beautiful thing, for it makes you the conscious creator of your own experience.

Still, to fully harness this power, you must master a few key mental faculties:

a. **Discriminating Intelligence**: Unlike animals, humans have the capacity to reflect, analyze, and distinguish between the real (Spirit/the unchanging) and the unreal (the phenomenal world/the constantly changing). This ability to discern is crucial for the spiritual journey, as it allows you to identify your true, unchanging nature (pure consciousness) from the temporary, fleeting contents of your experience. When you can see the difference, you prevent the 'unreal' circumstances of the world from dictating your mental state and actions. This power of discernment is a capability unique to humans. It is what separates your subjective experience from the function of any tool or machine, even those powered by AI.

b. **Concentrated Attention**: Attention is an earnest direction of the mind. Science is clear that multitasking doesn't work; it is an illusion of productivity that ultimately requires diminished mental effort. Because it trains your brain to quickly switch between tasks rather than focus on one. This constant switching results in errors, delayed responses, and a failure to truly connect with the immediate moment. Think of a conversation: when a person attempts to multitask while listening, their responses are often delayed, and they frequently ask for repetition or completely misunderstand the point. This is very noticeable these days as so many are preoccupied with what they are doing on their phones. And the conscious attention they are able to give to others can only be diminished.

The authority for this inefficiency is found in cognitive science: We can only consciously pay attention to a finite and remarkably small amount of information at any given moment. Psychologists refer to this as the **attentional bottleneck,** suggesting that the brain can typically only process four to seven discrete units of information at once in its working memory. This physiological limit means that when you believe you are multitasking, you are merely forcing your brain to rapidly switch tasks, scattering the available Spiritual Energy, **as opposed to keeping it focused,** and preventing the focused application required for Self-Mastery.

Concentration, the ability to maintain sustained attention on a single task, is a **mental muscle** that must be cultivated through practice. The ability is inherent, but it must be developed. By consciously focusing on one thing at a time, you will naturally improve your capacity to concentrate, leading to genuine, focused power.

c. **Knowledge and Understanding**: As Francis Bacon said, "knowledge is power." However, knowledge alone is not the power; it is in the **application** of that knowledge that creates power. As you integrate your knowledge and develop your inner awareness, you gain discernment—an unshakable inner certainty. You move beyond simply learning facts to an **absolute knowing**, where you become consciously aware of your own innate wisdom. This inner knowing guides you to the precise, perfect action (or inaction) required for success.

d. **Perseverance**: This word comes from the Latin perseverantia, meaning "steadfastness" or "constancy." Perseverance is the mental and emotional fortitude to keep moving forward, viewing obstacles not as roadblocks but as challenges to be overcome. It is about maintaining a course of action even when the desired outcome isn't immediately apparent.

e. **Selflessness**: Selflessness is the quality of caring for the well-being of others and acting to benefit them, often with little or no concern for personal gain. It is closely related to the concept of **altruism**, which is unconditional giving—another way of saying Love. Self-less individuals tend to be highly empathetic and are often willing to share their time, resources, skills, and emotional support without expecting anything in return.

f. **The Transmutation of Energy**

The Transmutation Exercise is the ultimate application of the Active Force—it is the process of consciously converting negative emotional energy (fear, anger, worry) into positive, constructive energy (focus, determination, love). This practice harnesses the power of your inner world by redirecting the powerful energy of the Sympathetic Nervous System (SNS) away from reaction and toward creation.

Take Immediate Action: The transmutation is completed through action. Direct the feeling into the newly chosen constructive endeavor. And keep trying; you'll get it!

As a powerful affirmation to fuel this transmutation, consider the words attributed to the great inventor, Nicola Tesla:

"I am one with the source. The universe flows through me.

 All that I need is already mine."

The Now and The End

A key component for progress and success is to consistently focus your attention on the good and the positive. Cultivating conscious awareness is all about strengthening your ability to **"pay attention"** and building your concentration muscle. This practice of keeping your mind **"in the now"** may seem to conflict with the concept of **"living in the end"**—the practice of imagining and feeling your heart's desire as already fulfilled. But there is no contradiction.

The present moment is the only moment you have to create. It is never any other time than now. You do not try to project your mind into the future; rather, you anchor the feeling of the fulfilled desire into your **present state**. By doing so, you consciously activate the energetic and subconscious forces that move you toward your objective. Therefore, staying mentally present is the fundamental skill, and this practice is the direct path to manifesting the life you desire.

Conscious Awareness Discipline – Stage 3: Deliberate Intention

A. The Rationale: From Observation to Creation

Having established control over your body's movements and practiced the release of distractions, you are now ready for the most powerful discipline: **Conscious Focusing**.

The objective here is not just to observe your inner world, but to **intentionally impress a specific blueprint** upon your subconscious mind. You move from releasing what you don't want to focusing entirely on what you do want. Your sustained concentration on a specific, consciously chosen goal or desired state is the mechanism for coordinating the conscious and subconscious minds for creation.

B. Conscious Discipline – The Deliberate Intention

Choose one specific object of focus and hold it without allowing the mind to wander.

1. **Establish Your Objective** (The Blueprint) First, consciously choose your object of focus. This should be the desired outcome, goal, or creative intention you wish to realize.

It must be stated as a **clear, concise affirmation** (e.g., "My business is thriving") or represented by a simple, **vivid mental image** of the finished result.

The objective should be chosen with a **sense of joy** and conviction and should represent your highest purpose or current goal.

2. Enter the State

Perform the **Physical Stillness** (Stage One) and move into the Physical Relaxation (Stage Two) to achieve the **relaxed-but-alert state.**

3. Hold the Focus

Gently introduce your chosen objective (the affirmation or image) into your awareness.

Your task is to **hold this object in the center of your conscious attention** for the entire designated time (e.g., 15 to 30 minutes). Do not analyze the objective; simply **observe it, feel its reality, and sustain it.**

4. Practice the Return (Using the Flow)

Whenever your mind drifts or a distracting thought arises, do not engage it.

Instead, immediately use the **"Load the Leaf"** technique to gently release the distraction to the Universal Flow. Then, immediately and gently return your entire focus to your chosen objective.

The goal is not to have zero distractions, but to shorten the time between a distraction arising and the conscious return to your intention.

C. The Key to Coordination

Your ability to sustain this focused intention, excluding all else, demonstrates to your subconscious mind that this chosen objective is your absolute priority. This sustained, single-point concentration coordinates the conscious and subconscious minds to begin the process of internal and external realization.

3. The Spiritual Conduit: Your True Nature

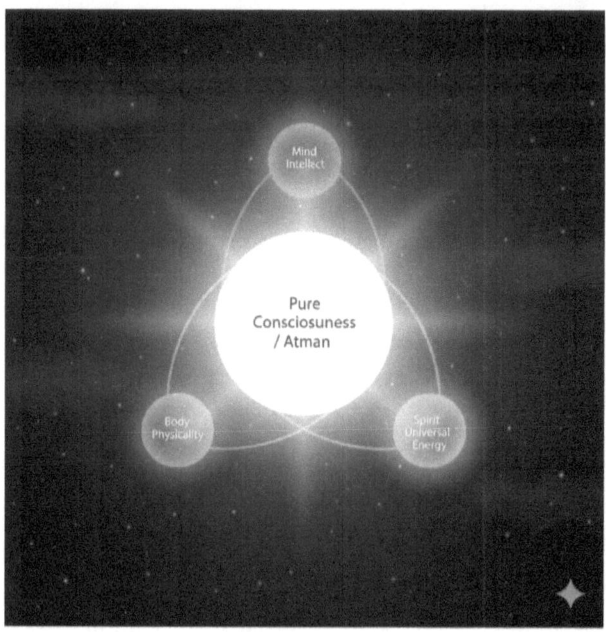

Figure 3.1

Figure 3.1 illustrates your true, limitless spiritual nature. The central sphere represents Pure Consciousness (Atman). The diagram illustrates how this central self includes three realms of experience—Mind, Body, and Spirit. It shows that true Self-Mastery is achieved through conscious, harmonious integration of all three aspects of being.

Foundation Uncovered: Ultimate vs. Empirical Reality

The concept you are about to encounter is arguably the most difficult yet the most rewarding idea in this book. It cannot be overstated; this idea is the hinge that supports the door to the freedom you will be entering. This powerful truth is achieved by employing a two-level model of reality and viewing the brain not as the producer of consciousness, but as a limiting instrument or reflector of a singular, fundamental Consciousness.

The Inner Mind is not merely a memory bank; it is the receptive faculty that connects you directly to the life force of the cosmos—the **Spiritual**

Energy. This energy is the source of all power, inspiration, and positive change, and is the current that governs your ability to manifest.

The Subjective Mind, or Inner Mind, accepts and transmits your **Intentional Will** to the limitless substance of the cosmos. It does this because, at the fundamental level of **Spiritual Energy**, *lack is an illusion and supply is boundless.* Your only true limitation is the quality of your desire and the strength of your belief.

Experiencing the Connection: While spiritual energy is universal, your experience of it is intensely personal. There is no right or wrong way to feel this connection. You may experience it as a physical sensation—a sudden rush of warmth or tingling. You may recognize its presence as pure inspiration, heightened hope, or clarity of intuition. When you connect with your spiritual energy, you will naturally feel more motivated, more deeply connected to others, and more harmonious with the world around you. This has always been true but now you begin to realize it.

Tuning In: You can strengthen your connection to this energy through dedicated Conscious Awareness Disciplines, such as Prayer, Meditation, or purposeful engagement with Nature and Art. The most important step is to simply remain open to the possibility of the existence of spiritual energy and allow your intuition to guide you, confirming that the power you seek resides within, as the very current of the **Universal Mind.**

This metaphysical concept is the collective consciousness that connects all beings, holding a vast pool of knowledge and wisdom accessible to everyone. It is the formless, spiritual energy behind all life, and this Universal Intelligence funnels into your being as pure consciousness with the inherent qualities of Love and wisdom. In essence, you are a walking, talking expression of this Love and wisdom—let it shine.

Your true nature therefore is spiritual. When you say, "I" that "I" is the part of you that is neither your body, your mind, nor your personality—is your direct connection to the Universal Mind. To begin to grasp this truth, we look to Advaita Vedanta, a Hindu philosophy which means "non-dualism." This school of thought states that an individual's body and mind are not separate from the outer world but are part of the same ultimate reality. Advaita Vedanta argues that the individual self is pure awareness that is mistakenly identified with the body and senses. In other words, you ARE reality. The Sanskrit maxim is **"That thou art,"** and its modern translation is clear: the "I" in you is the ultimate reality; you are that. This is a radical, life-altering idea, so it is perfectly natural you would want to sit with it a while and allow it to sink in. I suggest you do.

This perspective is achieved by employing a two-level model of reality and viewing the brain not as the producer of consciousness, but as a limiting instrument or reflector of a singular, fundamental Consciousness. Such a framework offers a powerful alternative for addressing the limitations of purely material science.

The two-level model helps address the "hard problem of consciousness," the question of why physical activity results in subjective experience. Since consciousness is not an object, not a physical thing, and is not even observable, many modern theories propose that the brain might not produce consciousness from scratch but rather acts as a receiver or filter for consciousness that exists more fundamentally in the universe. The simple fact that you still exist and wake up feeling rested after deep sleep—when the mind and personality are inactive—implies an underlying consciousness that persists during these states.

The apparent separation between your individual personality, your mind, and the external world is what Advaita calls the great illusion. This illusion arises when we mistakenly identify with the changing, temporary contents (the body, the mind, the personality) rather than the **unchanging witness**—pure consciousness.

To realize your true nature, then, is to understand that you are the ever-present, limitless, pure consciousness, beyond the temporary boundaries of mind and personality. You are not a human being having occasional **spiritual experiences,** but a spiritual being having a human experience.

The Responsibility of Truth

The profound teachings of non-dualism carry a unique responsibility. While the ultimate reality is that you are the unchanging, pure consciousness (**Brahman**), it is crucial to understand this truth within the context of your human experience. The body and mind exist within **empirical reality**, the world that is observable, measurable, and verified through your five senses. This is the **Realm of Effect**, and it comes with observable and measurable consequences. This wisdom is not a tool for spiritual bypassing. It does not mean that your experiences, emotions, pain, or psychological trauma should be ignored.

The fundamental truth is this: your inner thoughts and mental states are the **Cause**, and empirical reality is the **Effect**. We cannot escape the universal law that every action and thought has a corresponding consequence in the world of effect. All human experiences and ethical actions take place within this empirical reality, where your choices have tangible outcomes.

Furthermore, true realization does not lead to passivity; it leads to **compassionate, motivated action**. This external display of kindness and constructive effort is the most reliable feedback point—the gauge that assures you are correctly applying these spiritual principles and making true progress in this discipline. As you consistently apply the conscious awareness disciplines and integrate the principles found in this book, that compassionate, motivated action ceases to be a strenuous "have to" and becomes a natural, joyful "want to." The inner state you cultivate naturally expresses itself as effortless goodwill, bringing profound joy and ease to your life. This empowered action transforms your relationship with everything and ultimately allows improved harmony and a better empirical reality.

The Inner Wellspring

From a metaphysical standpoint, the **Ground of Being** refers to a fundamental ground of existence from which all things arise. This is called formless substance and contains the seeds of all possibilities. The Ground of Being is a source of infinite creative potential. Even in Quantum Mechanics, the concept of wave-particle duality and the observer effect suggests that reality is inherently indeterminate, and all possibilities remain open until they are observed or measured.

From the spiritual view, the divine and creative power is inherently within you, and you are within it. In the grand symphony of existence, the potential to compose a masterpiece is inherently within you. All you need is to be awakened to this potential. The profound realization of your connection to the divine power is the inevitable result of this awakening.

All people are inherently good and have the potential to achieve wonderful things. No matter your status or circumstances, all that matters is your state of mind and desire to do something constructive or creative with your life. You can do anything you choose to focus your mind on and are willing to show **PEP (personal effort and persistence)**. Want or desire is a powerful intrinsic driving force that can propel you beyond conscious limitations. It is why we ask the question: "what do I want" or "what is my purpose?"

The greatest "power" a human can achieve is **self-realization** according to Advaita Vedanta. This is the direct realization of the non-dual truth that you are the only reality, leading to liberation from suffering (moksha). However, that ultimate realization is not a gift or a mystical accident; it is the inevitable result of practical, daily effort. Having the knowledge is one thing, but to begin to apply it properly demands a diligent and fearless **inward appraisal** of your own character. Part of this inward looking includes confronting your mental conditioning and old ideas. If it is any consolation, you are not obligated to believe what others believe, or to live the way others might have you. Your spiritual life **grows** moment by moment through a **conscious and deliberate choosing, followed with intentional action.**

4. The Indispensable Purpose

"Thought, concentrated on a definite purpose becomes power."— Charles F. Haanel

To truly harmonize with the cosmos and create a life of profound meaning and impact, one vital element is essential: a clear, unwavering purpose. A **definite chief aim**, as Napoleon Hill identified in his 20-year study of success, was primary and the first step to achieving anything.

Without this guiding purpose, you risk becoming a musician without a gig. A clear and definite purpose is a vital force; without it, you will simply drift, and your potential will go unfulfilled. You have the power to accomplish any definite purpose you focus on because a clear purpose is a concentrated thought that becomes the cause for your reality.

To begin, write it down. Be specific about what you want to manifest, be definite in your aim, and focus on it. Seek to serve a higher purpose. Do what you love and what you are enthusiastic about. The most important thing is to consistently feel as though you are contributing to the greater good.

That, my friend, is success. It's the feeling of aligning your actions with your values and witnessing meaningful progress toward a specific goal. Success is not just the final accomplishment; it lies in the progress itself. When you focus on these small, consistent wins, you generate incredible momentum, creating success after success—a principle often referred to as the **"snowball effect."**

Say the affirmation: **"I can be what I will to be."** Say it every day and hear yourself.

IV Intentional Will

In him we live and move and have our being." — Acts 17:28

Conscious will is the active force you apply to awaken to conscious living. It's the moment you stop being driven by your hidden mind and start intentionally choosing what your role is and aligning it with the source.

he **Intentional Will** is the active force required to bridge the gap between abstract thought and physical result. It requires focus, persistence, and an absolute conviction in the creative power of the mind. Wallace Wattles perfectly summarized this process when he stated: 'Mind overcomes environment and every other obstacle; and mind is the only creator there is. Nothing can be created before we know that it can be and then make the proper effort.' There is much logic to these words. They remind us that the Will is the mechanism that ensures our positive thinking is not passive dreaming, but purposeful action.

The Intentional Will must be exercised daily. It must be directed consciously and deliberately for you to grow in power and effectiveness. One of the most potent tools for this is the affirmation: **"I can be what I will to be."** This is not an empty saying or a passive wish; it is a profound declaration that directly engages and strengthens the Will.

The Practical Function of the "I"

The most vital component of this affirmation is the word **"I."** As we stated in the Introduction, this **"I"** is not your conditioned personality, but the essence of your being that is **one with the Universal Mind.**

The practical function of this affirmation is two-fold:

Identity Reinforcement: While repeating the statement, you must consciously realize *who* is speaking. It is the infinite spiritual power within you—the true **"I"**—that is giving the command. This repetition deepens the belief that your inner self possesses the capability to manifest any desire. The more you say it with this recognition, the more it is believed, and the stronger your Will becomes.

Muscle Building: The phrase serves as a direct mental exercise that channels the Universal Energy, developing the focus, clarity, and persistence required for the Will to transform thought into reality.

1. Willingness: The Cooperative Force

Willingness is the only true requirement for deciding to act. It isn't just a desire to get to the summit; it's being ready to start climbing, even with heavy gear and an uncertain path. This distinction is crucial: wanting is a desire, while willingness is a readiness to engage. When you are willing, you are in a state of **cooperation with the Universal Source**.

Willingness is the key to unlocking harmony, alignment, and transformation in your life, providing the forward momentum to overcome self-doubt.

Follow the Director's Lead

You are a channel for infinite energy, a unique expression of the Universal Mind. While you have the freedom to think and act as you will, you are not the director. As my old friend used to say, "There is something around here that has the last word, and it's not me." This simple truth reveals a liberating idea: you don't have to control everything. The greatest freedom comes from trusting the flow and acting in harmony with the current of Universal Intelligence. Your crucial role is to align your will with the Director's, not to tell the Director how the scene should unfold. As the famed football coach Bill Belichick drove home to his players, "DO YOUR JOB!"

Remember, circumstances are a result of your thinking. Your thoughts prompt actions, which in turn create your reality. Your job is not to be ruled by circumstances, but to adjust yourself to them. By willingly accepting things as they are, you align your mindset with the present moment, allowing a new path to reveal itself. The willingness to learn from your circumstances is the key to accepting them, and only through that acceptance can you move forward.

2. Intentional Action: (PEP) Personal Effort and Persistence

Ultimately, your will is the motive power behind all manifestation. If you truly desire something, you will be eager and enthusiastic. So, how do you harness this power? Start by asking yourself, "Will I do this?" If your answer is yes, then put some **PEP** into it—**P**ersonal **E**ffort and **P**ersistence. Act with conviction and determination, knowing there is no room for doubting. Saying you can't means you won't, a helpful antidote for making excuses or procrastination.

Go all in. You can dabble, but the results will be equal to the amount of effort you put into it. When you act, you are sending a powerful signal to the universe that you are worthy of receiving what you desire. This effort isn't about frantic action; it's about calm, deliberate, and purposeful movement that flows directly from your inner state of alignment.

Say the affirmation: "I can, and I will!" And be emphatic, determined; I CAN AND I WIL!

3. The Unwavering Trust: Faith

Once you've aligned your will with the director's lead and embraced the guidance of willingness, you arrive at the heart of action. Faith means acting with confidence. When you act in faith, it is effortless because it is rooted in your spiritual nature. It bypasses the struggle and doubt of the ego and operates from a place of certainty. The true power lies not in the action itself, but in the **conscious conviction** and mindset, or confident expectation, which guides the action. And don't look back; faith is all about moving forward.

Faith is not surrendering; it's about being in **active cooperation** with a higher power. When you are actively cooperating you are in harmony with it. Trust is the motive power that animates your will, leading to the effortless manifestation of your desires. In the end, faith moves mountains, but you still must bring a shovel—make the effort and **trust** in the power that guides you. Remember, conscious, deliberate, and intentional action is where your power comes from. The days of living on auto- pilot are in the past.

a. **Be the Lighthouse**

The lighthouse doesn't seek out ships to save; it simply radiates light. So, be the lighthouse and let your light shine. When you live in a state of faith and spiritual alignment, you don't chase after things. Instead, your inner light attracts opportunities, people, and experiences that are in harmony with your thought vibrations.

b. **The Unwavering Test**

The greatest test of your unwavering trust comes when the physical evidence contradicts your goal. This is the point where most people retreat. Unwavering trust, however, is unconditional. It is the absolute certainty that your inner conviction is the ultimate reality, and the outer world must eventually conform.

Persistence Always Pays

The universe operates under a principle of absolute **accountability**. It registers and rewards every positive effort, regardless of past failures or intermittent success. It assures that no positive effort is ever truly wasted. In other words, it gives you credit for every effort and every success no matter how minute it might be. There is an old saying that goes: If at first you don't succeed, try, try again. Keep going because:

Your Effort is Never Wasted: Every attempt you make, every hour you study, every skill you practice, or every positive thought you hold is a deposit into your personal bank of success. This Law is so exact that it cannot ignore or erase a single positive contribution.

Success is Cumulative: That "intermittent" effort isn't scattered energy; it's a **cumulative force**. Even if you fail nine times, the tenth attempt benefits from the experience, data, and mental strengthening of the first nine. You are never starting from zero; you are starting from experience. 'Starting over' is an option, but it is never a necessity.

The Power of Small Victories: You don't need a flawless streak. Because the Law is absolute, it guarantees a credit for every moment you chose to stand up and try again. **The moment of effort is the moment of success.**

Failure is Simply Feedback: Don't view a setback as a sign to quit; view it as a **temporary pause** and a **learning opportunity**. Because the universe is perfectly just, you are guaranteed to receive the benefit of your focused efforts.

Therefore, **never give up hope or quit trying**, because the success you've earned with your effort is already accounted for and is on its way to materializing. The law of effort guarantees credit on every deposit you've made.

Therefore, by consistently showing up in life and doing your inner work, you align your will with the flow of the universe. In this way, you can hold the principle of "never give up!" not as a command to endlessly fight circumstances, but as a steadfast commitment to your spiritual purpose. Besides, you have every reason to keep trying to improve, learn, and succeed. Life is not a strategic and seriously sustained game of chess; it is a thrilling game of the unfolding of right thinking, good intent, and cooperation with the Universal Mind.

As we conclude this chapter on the power of unwavering focus and the disciplined pursuit of your highest self, I want to share a personal reflection. Early in my own spiritual journey, during a time of significant personal challenge, a wise spiritual advisor—who has since passed—recommended a small book to me: Jonathan Livingston Seagull by Richard Bach. At the time, my mind was clouded, and much of its message eluded me. Yet, my advisor simply told me, "Keep trying."

It took years for the deeper truths of that allegorical tale to fully unfold, but its essence resonates profoundly with the path we explore here. Jonathan was no ordinary seagull; he was an outcast who tirelessly pursued perfection in flight, not for food or status, but for the sheer joy of understanding and transcending his own limits. His journey taught three invaluable lessons that are central to achieving cosmic harmony and **Absolute Freedom**:

The relentless pursuit of excellence is its own reward: True mastery comes from within, driven by an unyielding desire to know and express your highest potential, even when misunderstood by others.

Limits are self-imposed illusions: What appears to be a boundary is merely a starting point for further growth. The pursuit of "what is" always reveals a deeper layer of truth and capability.

To truly live is to break free from the conditioned mind: Jonathan's greatest triumph was not just his extraordinary flight, but his liberation from the flock's conventional thinking, embodying the very essence of freedom and conscious living. This simple story became a profound reminder that the spiritual journey is one of continuous effort, guided by an inner knowing, toward ever-expanding horizons of self-discovery.

RICHARD BACH

JONATHAN LIVINGTON
LIVINGSTON SEAGULL

A STORY

V The Seven Universal Laws of Change and Influence

This chapter introduces the fundamental rules that govern how energy, **thought**, and matter move and interact in the universe. Thought is the *precursor* to **Energy** and **Matter**. Your individual mind is a reflection of this Universal Mind, and by focusing and changing your thoughts, you directly influence the mental blueprint of your reality, thereby shaping your energy and attracting corresponding matter (manifestation).

We often feel like passive recipients of life's circumstances, but these seven laws reveal the **mechanism** behind everything we experience. They are not mystical concepts; they are the immutable laws that explain why your conscious intention has power to shape your experience.

The wisdom contained here is derived from **The Kybalion**, a text compiled in the early 20th century summarizing the ancient **Hermetic Philosophy.** These principles have been studied for centuries and are essential keys for understanding how to consciously co-create.

By acknowledging these laws and understanding them, you gain a unique ability to shift your perspective from a passive participant to an **active influencer.** Possessing this knowledge and acting in accordance with these universal laws is the difference between blindly relying on luck, or fate and confidently wielding the tools necessary for sustained personal growth and abundance. They are part of the overall scaffolding upon which you are building your new life of alignment and flow. This knowledge is the key to being in cosmic harmony and finding freedom from circumstances and want; and all the while witnessing your own personal transformation. It is all about experiences and having a better understanding of what that experience is.

The Foundation: Mentalism and Correspondence

This ancient wisdom is now finding a home in modern science, particularly among theoretical physicists and philosophers who are discussing the idea that **consciousness is fundamental to reality**. This is a challenging concept to grasp, but it has a profound implication: that mind and consciousness are primary, while **matter is a secondary manifestation of mental energy.**

Consequently, if the universe is fundamentally mental, then **thoughts possess creative potential.** This means your inner state influences your external reality, shaping your experiences and the world around you. This suggests that thoughts operate under natural laws. Therefore, it's crucial to recognize the power of your own mind and take responsibility for the thoughts you cultivate. There is a spiritual axiom which states: where I am upset, there is something wrong with me. This leads to a difficult but essential lesson: you are upset; but your first task would be to quiet that disturbance within rather than react to it by blaming another. The issue likely originates within yourself anyway. By understanding that your reality reflects your consciousness, you can take control of your experiences rather than feeling like a victim of external circumstances.

Moreover, this perspective can be a source of great relief and empowerment. Instead of viewing yourself as a passive participant in a random world, you can understand that everything—including all matter, energy, and life—is a mental creation within the **Universal Mind** or universal consciousness. This foundational concept fundamentally shifts your perspective, revealing a profound truth: our reality isn't something that happens to us, but a manifestation of what is happening within us. It is our inner world that is the true and sole source of our reality. This realization empowers us to see that we are not merely products of our circumstances, but the creators of them.

The Law of Mentalism is your reminder that you are a creator. By consciously focusing on positive thoughts, you exercise your power to create a positive and connected world for yourself.

"As a man thinketh in his heart, so is he." — Proverbs 23:7

1. Law of Mentalism: The Unity of All Things

"The All is mind; the universe is mental." — The Kybalion

While The Law of Mentalism asserts the universe is fundamentally a mental creation, quantum physics provides a powerful scientific parallel to this law. This is the truth that ancient mystics and now modern scientists are beginning to explore: that everything is connected.

This interconnectedness isn't just a metaphor; it's a scientific fact. **Quantum entanglement** is a wild but very real phenomenon where particles become so deeply linked that they share the same destiny, *no matter how far apart they are.* As Einstein put it, this is "spooky action at a distance." Imagine a pair of coins spinning together in perfect sync. No matter how far apart you separate them, if one lands on heads, you know with absolute certainty that the other has landed on tails, instantly. The properties of each particle influence each other—a direct testament to the deep, unseen unity of the universe.

This scientific reality directly supports the spiritual idea that the All is One. Your inner world and outer reality are not separate; they are profoundly linked, just like those entangled particles. Your thoughts, emotions, and intentions, when directed with conscious will, send out a ripple that is connected to the whole.

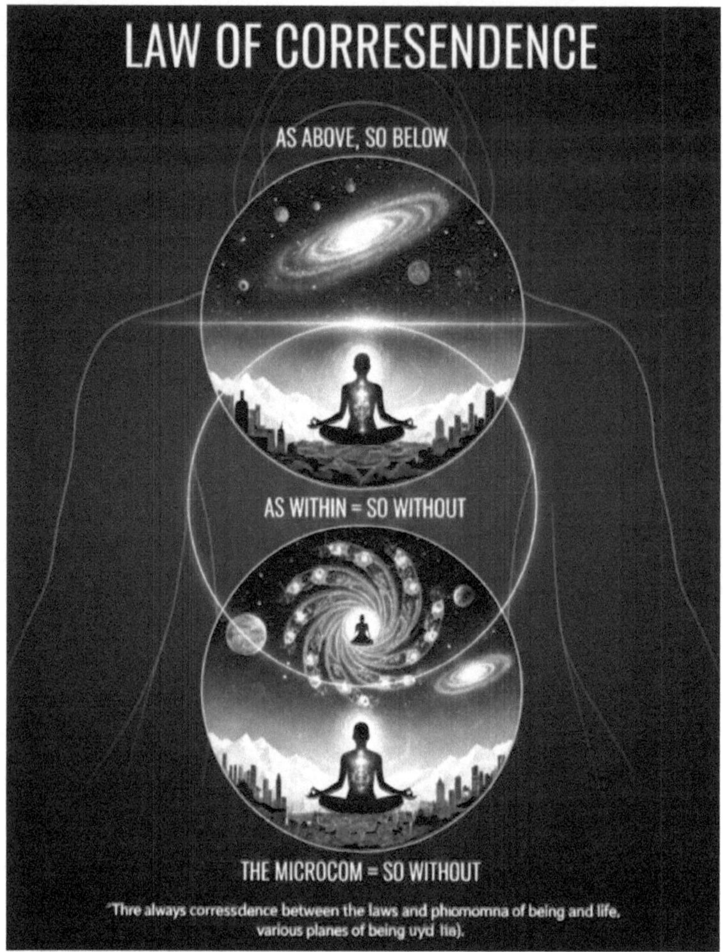

The Template and the Reflection

The Principle of Correspondence states, **"As above, so below; as below, so above."**

There is always a correspondence between the governing laws and **phenomena** (the observable facts, events, and occurrences) that manifest on a given plane of existence. These **appearances**, or manifestations, are seen across the various planes: **Spiritual, Mental, and Physical**. This means the patterns of the **macrocosm** (the universe/spirit) are consistently reflected in the patterns of the microcosm (humans/atoms/matter).

This is one of the most fundamental principles, as it ties all planes of existence together. It assures you that the very same spiritual laws governing the creation of galaxies are active within your consciousness. The inner structure of your thoughts, beliefs, and emotional patterns dictates the outer structure of your life. **The mind is the template, and the world is the reflection.**

This principle reveals the vital connection between the planes: your **inner world** (thought/energy) is mirrored in your **outer world** (matter/experience). By understanding the rules on the physical plane, you can infer rules on the mental and spiritual planes, and vice versa. By mastering the laws of your inner world, you gain influence over the laws of your outer world.

3. Law of Cause and Effect: Thought is Cause

Nothing happens by chance. In the grand tapestry of existence, every thread is interwoven, **every action begets a reaction, and every effect has its cause.** This fundamental truth, the Law of Cause and Effect, is the very engine of your reality. It is the detached mechanical law of the universe and at the heart of this engine lies your own **mental signature.**

Your Mental Signature: The Dominant Cause

Your mental attitude is unique to you, and it leaves an undeniable imprint on your reality. Think of it like this: just as a fingerprint is unique to an individual, your mental signature is the distinctive pattern of your inner world. It is the prevailing quality of your thoughts, the dominant emotional tone you carry, and the deep-seated beliefs that shape your perception.

This mental signature is an active, influential force—a thought force. It is not about a fleeting thought, but the consistent, underlying current—the default setting—of your consciousness. This is the inner landscape from which your intentions spring, your decisions are made, and your reactions are formed. It is a silent, powerful force that acts as the primary **cause** for what you ultimately observe and experience in your life.

A foundational principle of metaphysics and philosophy holds that your thoughts obey natural law. This assertion, most clearly articulated in the principle of **Mentalism** (The All is Mind; The Universe is Mental), means your thoughts are governed by the same Law of Cause and Effect as everything else in the universe. In essence, what you consistently hold in your mind eventually finds its way into your experience. Are you looking for the good in others or looking for trouble? You will find what you are looking for, I have no doubt about that.

Consequently, you owe it to yourself to substitute constructive and positive attitudes for destructive and negative thinking. This is not about being a victim; it's about acknowledging your power. The aim is to learn how to actively shape your mental signature, thereby harmonizing with Cosmic Intelligence itself.

Words: The Vibration of Thought

Words are not just sounds; they are a direct extension of your thoughts and feelings. They are the tangible expression of your inner world. Words carry meaning, and they are profoundly impactful especially when conveyed with feeling. For this very reason, you must be mindful of your words and your intent when you speak. Words are not separate from your mental signature; they are its direct broadcast. **Think before speaking and speak with the same sentiment you would have another speak to you.** The words you use are not just communication; they are a powerful act of creation.

Conscious Awareness Discipline: Shifting Your Mental Signature

To begin shifting your mental signature, try this simple practice:

Check-In: Periodically throughout your day, take a moment to pause. Ask yourself: **What is my predominant mental attitude right now?** Am I in a state of gratitude, frustration, or calm?

Observe without Judgment: Do not criticize yourself for the feeling you find. Simply observe it as a witness. This builds the muscle of awareness—no judgment.

Choose a New State: This can be the most difficult, perhaps. But you must consciously choose a new state of mind. For example, if you find yourself feeling frustrated, gently guide your thoughts toward something you can be grateful for. Or when angry, think about the person as an equal and entitled to respect and gentle consideration. I know that's how I like to be treated. You will find this remedy to be highly beneficial as it also serves as a great stress release.

Anchor with a Word: Use a word as an anchor. Silently repeat "peace" or "calm" to yourself. This acts as a signal to your mind and body to shift to a new frequency.

By consistently applying this practice, you can actively shape your mental signature and invite harmonious experiences into your life. This impact cannot be overstated.

The Universal Laws are impartial, impersonal, and mechanical; they execute based on the intended thought presented, not on merit or worthiness. As Haanel clearly states: **'The creative power of thought is impersonal and your ability to think is your ability to control it and make use of for the benefit of yourself and others.'** This reveals our ultimate responsibility: the power itself is neutral, but the thinker is not. Therefore, the highest application of these laws is achieved when your Intentional Will is directed toward service and contribution, not solely for personal gain.

4. Law of Vibration: The Mechanics of Attraction

"Nothing rests, everything moves, everything vibrates." The Kybalion

Everything in the universe is in a constant state of motion. This includes you. Nothing rests; everything vibrates at a specific frequency. This fundamental law states that thoughts, emotions, and everything else are forms of energy. Just as radio broadcast on a specific frequency to receive a signal, you are constantly broadcasting along your own unique frequency and attracting the corresponding experiences—**your received signals.**

Your Vibrational Frequency: The Engine of Attraction

Your thoughts and emotions are not just fleeting mental events; they are real energy that controls the vibration of your being. This is the **Law of Vibration** at its most personal level. When you hold thoughts with intention and emotion, you send out a powerful signal that influences the world around you.

Moreover, **Thought** is high-frequency energy, while **Matter** is energy vibrating at an incredibly low frequency. The movement and interaction between any two things (including your thought and the thing you desire) is determined by their **resonance**; like vibrations attract (Law of Attraction), which is why changing your emotional/thought frequency is necessary to change your material results.

This is the driving force behind the **Law of Attraction**. The Law of Attraction is the principle that like energy attracts like energy. The Law of Vibration is the engine, and the Law of Attraction is the result. Whatever you hold in your conscious and subconscious mind with consistent emotion and focus—whether it is positive or negative—will set the frequency that attracts your experiences.

The Practice of Gratitude: Raising Your Frequency

To raise your frequency and attract more of what you desire, an attitude of gratitude is the keynote. Gratitude is a powerful state of being. Yes, it feels good when you are grateful but only when you act on it. Gratitude must be actively demonstrated; it is something you do. And even a little goes a long way.

It's also important to remember that gratitude is not exclusively for positive circumstances. Negative circumstances can be blessings in disguise. It may not be what you want, but it may be something you need, or, in some cases, something you do not need. The key is to look beyond the unpleasant things and find the good. From there, you can move forward constructively, creating a more harmonious environment. Ultimately, a grateful heart leads to good health, happiness, and prosperity. Gratitude is a powerful state that fundamentally changes your vibration which in turn changes your experience.

Having an attitude of gratitude is like chicken soup for the mental state. It provides so much goodness.

Conscious Awareness Discipline: Practicing Gratitude

You can feel good at any time by practicing gratitude in your daily life with the following:

Gratitude Journal: Everyday, write down three to five things you are genuinely grateful for, no matter how small. This trains your brain to look for the good in your life. And don't forget the bow on top, the breath that gives you life.

The A-B-C Method: When you encounter an unpleasant situation (A), consciously choose a grateful response (B), and take action to find the good in it (C). This trains your mind to habitually look for the positive—a more constructive way to move forward.

Verbalize Your Gratitude: Make a conscious effort to thank people. Express your appreciation to a coworker, family member, or friend. This reinforces the feeling of gratitude and radiates positive energy. By consciously practicing gratitude, you deliberately raise your vibration, becoming a powerful magnet for the life you desire.

The following poem is From <u>The Law of Mentalism</u> by A. Victor Segno. And it encapsulates most of this book.

<u>The Power of Thought</u>

"I hold it true that thoughts are things
Endowed with bodies, breath, and wings,
And that we send them forth to fill
The world with good results- or ill.

That which we call our secret thought,
Speeds to the earth's remotest spot,
And leaves its blessings or its woes,
Like tracks behind it as it goes."

We awaken in another
Just the thoughts our minds contain.
If we're kind we win their kindness,
If we hate, they hate again.

We pass on to brother mortals
The vibration of the soul,
And the knowing ones receive them,
As they search from pole to pole."

We build our futures thought by thought,
Or good or bad- and know it not.

Thought is another name for fate,
Choose, then, thy destiny and wait-
For Love brings Love and hate brings hate."

5. Law of Gender: The Two Forces of Creation

All creation requires a union of two forces, which the Law of Gender names the **Masculine and Feminine principles**. This law states that **"Gender is in everything; everything has its Masculine and Feminine Principles."** This is not about biological sex, but about the active and receptive forces inherent in all energy.

The Masculine Principle is the Active Force—the Will, the projection of desire, the energy of asking and demanding. It is the focused, purposeful movement of consciousness.

The Feminine Principle is the Receptive Force—Imagination, the capacity for believing and receiving. It is the nurturing space where the mental seed is held, grown, and manifested into form.

These two principles must work in harmony to create your desired reality. Your Intentional Will (Masculine) must act with firm purpose, and your Imagination (Feminine) must be open and receptive to the universe's provision. Without the Active Will, the Receptive Imagination remains dormant. Without the Receptive Imagination, the Active Will has no blueprint to follow.

The Manifestation Formula: Ask, Believe, Receive

The Law of Gender established the Masculine Principle (Asking) and the Feminine Principle (Receiving) as the two required forces for creation. And we come to the simple, three-step formula for manifestation:

Ask: The Power of Earnest Desire (Masculine Force) First , know what your aim is. You must know what you want with such clarity and conviction that you literally petition for it. The clarity and sincerity of your asking is the first step in the process of creation. When you know what you want, write it down. Be clear, definite, and specific.

Believe: Confident Expectation (cooperation) The second and most crucial step is to believe that what you desire is already yours. Neville Goddard calls this **"living in the end."** This means assuming your wish has already been fulfilled. Your thought frequency needs to be in tune with the frequency of your desire as if it has already manifested. To attract good things, you need to feel good, feel the joy, the relief, and the gratitude of having it now.

Receive: Take Ownership (Feminine Force) Substance takes form according to mental demand; but your job is not to inform the Absolute as to how or when your desire will manifest. Your only role is to demonstrate that you are ready to receive by being in the correct frame of mind and acting accordingly. The universe will provide. Your role is to show up and remain open to every possibility life presents.

The Law of Attraction is the magnetic principle of the Universe; it ensures that like energy attracts like energy. To put it simply: **We attract into our lives the things we focus on.** This is why mental discipline and the ability to sustain positive mental attention are not merely side practices, but absolute necessities for conscious creation. What you hold in your dominant mental picture will eventually find its way into your circumstance.

Once you understand these laws, you realize the power of consistent mental attitude. Charles Haanel, in The Master Key System, observed this principle in action, stating that **'much gathers more is true on every plane of existence.'** This is the nature of accumulation: a positive, expectant mental state attracts and compounds favorable conditions, just as negative thinking will eventually compound loss. When you direct your Will with clarity, you ensure that you are gathering 'more' of what serves your highest good.

The universe is built on constant creation and limitless resource. **The law of abundance** is a natural law of the universe. It means supply is never the problem; the flow is always constant. The only block to abundance is any limiting belief the mind has been conditioned to accept. When you align your thoughts with this fundamental truth, you cooperate with the universe's natural state of abundance.

Imagination: The Feminine Blueprint

Your imagination is the greatest tool you possess in this process. It is your mental workshop where you can create the blueprint for your reality before it has even appeared in the physical world. The process of using your imagination to create your desired reality is called **visualization**.

How to Use Your Imagination as a Tool: The act of visualizing is not just about seeing pictures in your mind. It is about creating a sensory and emotional experience.

Create the Blueprint: Just as an architect first envisions a building in their mind, you must first create a mental blueprint of what you desire. Get specific. What do you want to accomplish? What does it look and feel like to have it already?

Add Feeling: The Power of Emotion: The power of imagination is amplified by emotion. It's not enough to just see the picture; you must **feel it**. As you visualize, tap into the feelings of joy, gratitude, and relief that you would experience as if your desire is already yours. This feeling-state is the powerful magnet that attracts your desire to you.

Engage the Senses: Make your visualization as real as possible by engaging all your senses. What do you hear? What do you smell? What do you taste? By adding these layers, you make the mental image so real that your subconscious mind begins to accept it as an existing reality.

Visualizing your achieved goal is not about hoping for a future event; it's about making your desired reality so tangible in your mind that it begins to manifest in your life. Athletes use visualization as a tool for improving performance. An all-star and world champion major league pitcher once said, "Visualize, visualize, visualize- then go for it."

The Remaining Principles: Polarity and Rhythm

In this chapter, we explored five of the seven fundamental laws governing the universe: Mentalism, Correspondence, Cause and Effect, Vibration, and Gender.

The two remaining Hermetic Principles

The Law of Polarity and the Law of Rhythm are crucial to navigating the human experience.

THE LAW OF POLARITY
Everything is Dual. All Opposites are One

The Law of Polarity: deals with duality—the truth that all things exist on a spectrum (e.g., love/hate, light/dark) and that opposites are merely two extremes of the same thing.

THE LAW OF RHYTHIM
Everything Flows Out and In. All Things Rise and Fall.

The Law of Rhythm is the cyclical nature of life, the flow and ebb, the rise and fall of all things.

Because these two laws specifically address the emotional and psychological challenges of personal growth and character, their integration and practical application will be explored in depth within Chapter VI (The Moral Mind) and Chapter VIII (Maturity and Growth), respectively.

Another important scientific concept governing your power to create is the principle of perpetual transmutation of energy. This fundamental principle confirms that all energy is constantly in motion and can neither be created nor destroyed, only transformed from one state to another. It is through this perpetual cycle that the mental energy of your thoughts and intentional will are transmuted into physical reality, and latent cosmic energy is drawn into manifestation.

You actively participate in transmutation of energy by applying three key actions:

Conscious Focus: Your thoughts and emotions are powerful energy generators. By maintaining a predominant positive mental attitude, you create high-frequency energy that attracts positive experiences and outcomes.

Intentional Action: It is not enough to merely think about what you desire. You must take action toward your goals. When you take action, you are actively transmuting your thoughts and emotions into physical effort and, eventually, physical reality.

Self-Belief: Your belief is the necessary internal catalyst. When you fundamentally believe in yourself and your power to create, you send a powerful, high-frequency signal to the universe, accelerating the process of transmutation and assuring you are ready to receive what you desire.

The true value in studying these Universal Laws lies not in their intellectual complexity, but in their practical application to your life. The core benefit of knowing the laws is gaining Self-Mastery and a sense of Empowerment. Once you understand the mechanics of reality, from the Law of Mentalism to the Law of Cause and Effect—you are no longer a passive passenger in life. You become the conscious, capable architect of your circumstances, wielding the tools of creation with conscious and deliberate intent.

Affirmations: "As the plants grow, as the Earth moves and as the fruit ripens, so I bud, blossom, and receive." "I am open and receptive to all the abundance in the universe."

VI Moral Mind

The Necessity of Mental Housecleaning

The first step in transforming your dominant mental attitude is a comprehensive **mental housecleaning**. You must assess your internal landscape, which may feel difficult as it involves facing the adverse thoughts that have held you back. However, the purpose of this housecleaning is **two-fold,** based on the sound logic of conscious creation:

It allows you to identify and remove the **destructive thinking** (fear, doubt, worry) that is actively blocking the flow of Universal Energy.

More importantly, identifying the destructive patterns immediately helps you **recognize and employ the constructive ideal** that must take their place.

This process facilitates the change from useless, unconstructive thinking and your ability to demonstrate the ideal self you are trying to form. *To manifest an ideal, one must be able to think along those same ideal lines.* By clearly defining what you are not and simultaneously what you will be, you equip yourself with the improved thinking necessary to execute the plan received from the **Universal Mind.**

Your Inner Strengths and Challenges

My spiritual advisor and I were sitting in his office one morning, and I was complaining about people, which I did a lot. He said to me in his usual gentle manner, "People are not in this world to please you." His easy and matter-of-fact way of speaking made it somewhat palatable. Recognizing this fact was not a critique of others; You, I and everyone has 'stuff' on our minds, and we are not thinking of each other most of the time. It's okay, we have to give attention to ourselves. But to expect that others make concessions and adjustments to please us is not only unreasonable but unrealistic.

All I needed was a little bit of self-honesty to realize my own self-centeredness and how I needed to change. That took a while of course—not the realizing, but the changing. Considering that I had a mindset focused on lack, was full of fear but tried not to show it and had resentments galore, change was not going to be an overnight matter. Come to find out, it is a process, and a slow one at that. And we can only do it one day at a time.

I had to take a good, hard look at myself. It's difficult to have a healthy perspective and focus on abundance, contribute to society, and express love for your fellow man when one possesses none of these attributes and doesn't even realize it. Such attributes are acquired through daily practice and application of the principles in this book. There are only two directions for us: forward or backward. You either progress or regress; no one stands still. So, be a work in progress.

That said, growth doesn't have to be in leaps and bounds either and hardly ever is anyway. The watchword here then is progress. Even the smallest step forward or the smallest improvement is progress. You are not trying to get 'good;' you are already good. You were born that way. And at this point you are simply making an inward search for strengths of character and taking stock of them. This thorough look inward is necessary for spiritual growth. It is to be an honest and thorough self- appraisal.

Not an Overhaul, but an Awakening.

To be clear, engaging in this self-appraisal is not about declaring bankruptcy on your character. While some may indeed recognize the need for a complete overhaul, many others already strive to live by principles of integrity, humility, and high moral standards. If you fall into the latter group, you might be tempted to dismiss this work, thinking it unnecessary. This would be missing the ultimate purpose. The inventory is not merely a search for glaring faults; it is the deliberate development of **conscious awareness**, the ability to know your true self as you are, at this moment. This deeper self-knowledge is the wellspring of spiritual growth and the essential commitment toward achieving the **cosmic harmony** that is the promise of this book. Regardless of your current moral standing, this process is designed for you.

As you begin this process of honest introspection, it is essential to understand the principle that governs duality in all things: the **Law of Polarity**. This principle states, "Everything is Dual; everything has poles; everything has its pair of opposites." This law is the philosophical foundation for taking stock of yourself. It assures you that every character liability you possess is merely the negative pole of a strength you can cultivate. These poles are two extremes of the same inner quality, with countless degrees of change between them.

Conventionally, people view hate as the opposite of love. However, hate still requires energy and engagement. In truth, hate is a non-entity; it is merely the absence of a constructive force, holding no power in and of itself. The only one hurt by it is the hater.

The genuine opposite of Love, therefore, is **indifference**. Love is a verb; it is an activity and therefore is the active, unifying force of connection and will, while indifference is the total absence of that energy. It is a neutral, unfeeling void. Indifference is the ultimate extreme of the other end of the spectrum from love. By choosing to eliminate indifference and recognizing the non-power of hate, you choose to invest your energy exclusively in the creative pole: Love. More on Love later in the closing chapter. **For now, it is time to assess your moral position.** You will need to employ your intentional will to shift your vibration from the challenging, negative pole (e.g., resentment) toward the constructive, positive pole (e.g., peace and Love).

So literally, don't be afraid to take a look at yourself. Just as a business takes inventory of its stock, you want to do the same thing with your moral qualities, the character traits that are not visible to the outer world. You must document what you find for the growth and change process to be effective and lasting. Take a thorough look inward and be brave about it. You'll never become master of yourself if you cannot take a good look at your character traits, especially the glaring ones. Be gentle with yourself, too. You don't have to feel guilty about what you find or beat yourself up over anything. Remember, it's just an objective look, nothing to be afraid of.

You won't like seeing the liabilities, but you are not supposed to. This is the process by which you will be building and developing the moral character trait of **courage**.

In this moral inventory, you will discover both assets (strengths) and liabilities (challenges). You must look at all of it. This is about the identification of constructive, useful thinking and consequent behaviors while at the same time, eliminating destructive and useless ones.

1. Your Assets (Strengths)

We will ease into the process by first looking at strengths. For me, I found this to be the more difficult part. At first, I found it hard to notice my strengths due to low self-esteem, but acknowledging both strengths and weaknesses is crucial for a healthy and balanced reflection.

My first attempt at this, I remember writing down only the bad things I saw. I took it to be 'open season' on myself. It was natural for me to take aim at myself. I was full of guilt and accustomed to beating myself up. I also missed the point about it needing to be thorough. I was not afraid; I just wanted to get it over with, so I finished in about an hour. And when I brought it to my spiritual advisor for review, he took a quick look at it and said, "where's the rest of it"? Needless to say, I had only written the bad 'stuff.' So I had a second go at it and more things came to mind that needed to be included. If I can stress one thing here, it is not to skimp. Be as thorough in your inward search as possible. You will only have to do it once if done fearlessly and thoroughly from the start. Take as much time as needed; easy does it but do it as the saying goes.

Now, let's begin with a list of common assets.

Honesty- We have two types: There is "cash register" honesty, which means you simply don't steal. Then there is **honesty with oneself**, which means you don't kid yourself.

Respect: The true meaning of respect involves valuing and acknowledging the worth of others, their opinions, and their boundaries, and treating them with dignity and kindness. But before you can extend that to others, you must first treat yourself with respect. You must value your own worth. There is a great saying, "God doesn't make junk." Believe it! You are made in the divine image of your Creator. Not only that, but there is also only one of you. In that respect, you are a unique and special individual.

Being respectful involves these key actions: **active listening** (seeking to understand others' perspectives), **Support** (offering encouragement and assistance), **kindness** (being compassionate and considerate toward others), **politeness** (remembering 'please' and 'thank you'—manners do matter), and above all, **acknowledging boundaries** (showing respect for someone else's space and autonomy).

Compassion: This one is simple. If you can recognize when someone is suffering **AND you want to help**, then you have compassion.

Resilience: It is the ability to bounce back from adversity. It's spiritual strength; it allows you to face challenges, disappointments, and setbacks without giving up. We're concerned with growing through problems, not avoiding them. You have the inner resources to endure.

Moral Courage: Moral courage is the strength to do what is right, even when it is difficult or unpopular. It is about acting in accordance with your inner principles, even when it puts you at odds with the world around you. Just be true to yourself. I mean, why wouldn't you?

Reliability: Reliability is the consistency of your character. It means being dependable and trustworthy, keeping your word, and following through on your commitments. It is a fundamental building block of integrity and self-respect.

Responsibility: Responsibility is the ability to choose your response to life's circumstances. It is a powerful state that allows you to take ownership of your actions and thoughts, without blaming others or external circumstances.

Feel free to include in your own inventory any assets you feel I have left off the list.

2. Your Liabilities (Challenges)

Just as it is important to recognize your strengths, it is equally important to shine a light on the character traits that are holding you back. This is not about judgment, but about **awareness**. As if they aren't glaring enough, right? But by taking an honest look at your liabilities, you can begin to see them for what they are: adjustments in thinking and personal challenges to be overcome, not permanent flaws.

Fear: The way to overcome fear is by being consciously aware of power. Fear and resentment are not necessities; they are useless thoughts that must be eliminated. Fear must be destroyed, and there is a process to eliminate it and other negative and destructive thinking. While fear can have a necessary function for survival, unreasonable fears, if left alone, will eventually destroy you. So, it is necessary to face them squarely; and when you do, they no longer have any power over you. That is the divine paradox of courage, and it is a wondrous thing.

Scientific research suggests that humans are only innately born with two natural fears: the fear of loud noises and the fear of falling. This means that nearly every other anxiety you experience is fabricated and learned from society, conditioning, or past trauma. This truth is incredibly empowering: any fear that has been learned can be unlearned, making it a challenge you are inherently equipped to overcome. I find this to be welcoming encouragement.

Dishonesty: Dishonesty creates a barrier to spiritual growth, but its damage is much deeper. It corrupts your ability to discern truth, forcing you to live in a fictional reality constructed from half-truths and denial. This self-deception poisons every decision, relationship, and thought, leading to chaos and isolation. Ultimately, this denial prevents you from seeing your genuine self, which completely severs your connection from the Universal Source of truth and power. You will ultimately end up broken and powerless.

"This above all; to thine own self be true,

and it must follow, as the night the day,

thou canst not then be false to any man."

— From William Shakespeare's Hamlet

Selfishness: Selfishness is an over-concern with your own interests at the expense of others. It is the root of most negative character traits and is antithetical to living a spiritual life, which is based on unity, the act of giving and interconnectedness.

Irresponsibility: Irresponsibility is the tendency to blame others for your circumstances. It is a mindset that keeps you in a state of victimhood, robbing you of your power to choose your response and create your reality.

Negative Emotions: Emotions such as anger, resentment, jealousy, Self-pity, and guilt are destructive and corrosive. They lower your vibrational frequency and create a mental state that attracts negative experiences. Here you just need to recognize them. Remember, you possess the conscious will to dismiss guilt when it arises. In other words, don't stay feeling guilty for too long.

Disrespect: Disrespect for yourself and others reflects a lack of inner worth and an inability to see the divinity in others. It is a barrier to healthy relationships and spiritual alignment. You will need to start building self-respect from within. But it takes a concerted effort as I can attest to this personally.

The practice of taking stock of yourself (the moral inventory), is a vital step toward true and lasting peace of mind and joy. It is deeply personal and powerful, and you can begin the process with this simple exercise: a. Find a Quiet Space: You will want to be alone while you carry out this introspective task. b. Document Your Traits: Using a journal and a pen, make two columns. On one side, list your Assets (Strengths). On the other side, list your Liabilities (Challenges). Take as much time as you need—days if necessary. But do not procrastinate. Just do it as the famous Nike saying says. c. Observe Without Judgment: As you write, ignore any thoughts of fear, anger, doubt, or insecurity. When they appear, just ignore them. Give them no space to fester. The whole point of this is to be brave about it. You are building courage. d. Embrace the Truth: Your only job is to be honest with yourself. This process is not about beating yourself up; it is about shining a light on your inner world which automatically eliminates any darkness. In this way, you will be better able to rise above your shortcomings.

3. Cultivating Your Mental Ecosystem

With your moral inventory complete, the next **opportunity for improvement** requires **active effort** to cultivate a mental and physical environment that supports your high-vibration poles. Inventory was the foundation; these practices are the **active construction** of your new self and the reality you experience.

Your mental resources are the internal tools you possess to navigate life and maintain well-being, broadly categorized as **Cognitive, Emotional, Social, and Spiritual.** These faculties are interconnected and work together to ensure you thrive. The process is defined as 'out with the old and in with the new': consciously developing your improved self to enhance your overall health and well-being. .

a. Cognitive Mental Faculties

Attention - The ability to focus and process information selectively.

Memory: The ability to encode, store, and retrieve information.

Learning: The ability to acquire new knowledge and skills.

Problem-solving: The ability to analyze situations and develop solutions.

Decision-making: The ability to weigh options and make choices.

Creativity: The ability to think creatively and generate new ideas.

Here are some examples of how to cultivate these cognitive mental resources:

Stimulation: Engage in activities that stimulate your mind, such as reading, puzzles, and learning new things. Simply put, pursue your interests.

Focus: Practice mindfulness and meditation to improve your focus and self-awareness. This should already be part of your daily routine.

Physical Health: Get regular exercise to boost your mood and energy levels; and eat a healthy diet to support brain function. The two go hand in hand.

Connection: Connect with loved ones and build strong social relationships.

Seeking Help: Do not hesitate to seek professional help if you are struggling with your mental health. It's just the right thing to do, especially if you are struggling with something internally. You need to share the burden. I was always told that a problem shared is a problem cut in half. It certainly worked for me.

b. Emotional Wellness

Emotional wellness is rooted in **self-awareness** and **emotion regulation**. The goal here is not to eliminate difficult emotions, but to identify and feel them without immediate reaction. This is the true purpose of developing self-control, and completely necessary if you are to be the master of yourself. The charts that follow will aid you as you work on self-improvement.

Emotional health is maintained by the following:

Emotional Resource	Cultivation Tip
Self-Awareness & Identification	**Name It to Tame It**: Practice identifying your emotion in a single word (e.g., "I feel frustration," "I feel anxiety") without judgment. This simple act of identification is a form of allowing and creates mental distance.
Emotion Regulation	**The Three-Breath Pause**: When an emotion arises, consciously take three slow, deep breaths before deciding on your response. This trains your brain to create a gap between the feeling and the reaction, strengthening your **Resilience**.
Empathy	**Practice Active Listening**: To build empathy for others, commit to listening to another person for three minutes without interrupting or formulating your own response. Seek only to understand their perspective.

c. Social Well-being and Wellness

Social health is maintained through **Communication** and **People Skills**. Developing these skills is crucial for building the **Social Support** network you need for overall well-being.

Social Resource	Cultivation Tip
People Skills	**Communicate with Intent:** Before speaking, take a moment to ask: What is my goal? (e.g., to inform, to share Love, to set a boundary). This ensures your message is clear and effective, strengthening your People Skills. The more consciously aware you become, the better you will get at this.
Social Support	**Be the Initiator:** Don't wait for others to reach out. Once a week, commit to being the active source of connection—text or call a loved one just to check in, without needing anything in return. This strengthens the entire network.

d. Nurturing Your Spiritual Alignment

Spiritual health is maintained through a sense of **Meaning** and **Purpose**, **Hope**, and **Connection** to something larger than yourself. These are the practices that nurture the soul. The following table is an example of a few helpful tips for cultivating and nurturing your spiritual condition. You may have some thoughts of your own as you grow and learn a few tips you can use in your daily life. The ones that follow are some examples:

Spiritual Resource	Cultivation Tip
Meaning and Purpose	**The Why Statement:** Write a single sentence defining why you are on this journey (e.g., "I seek peace to better serve my family"). Review this statement daily to align your actions with your purpose.
Hope & Connection	**Gratitude or Prayer:** Spend five minutes either journaling specific things you are grateful for or engaging in prayer. This practice builds **Hope** by focusing on the positive and strengthens your **Connection** to the Universal Source.

Conscious Awareness Discipline – Stage 4: Ideal Self-Concept Integration

A. The Rationale: From Goal to Identity

While Stage 3 focuses on creating external results (goals), Stage 4 focuses on **internal transformation**. True, lasting achievement is built upon the foundation of a new identity. This discipline is the intentional practice of embodying your *Ideal Self*—the person you are striving to become—in areas of character, emotion, and discipline. This integration allows the subconscious mind to align your daily behaviors with your highest identity.

B. Conscious Discipline – Ideal Self Integration

Practice sustained concentration on the *qualities* and *feelings* of your ideal future self.

1. Establish Your Ideal Self (The Identity)

Before beginning, **consciously choose the qualities of the self you wish to integrate.** This is not about achieving a specific material goal, but about character and being. Examples include:

Emotional State: *I am calm and in control of my feelings.*

Mental Strength: *I am mentally resilient and see challenges as opportunities.*

Discipline: *I embody consistent discipline in my daily habits.*

2. Enter the State

Perform the **Physical Stillness (**Stage 1) and Physical Relaxation (Stage 2) to achieve the **relaxed-but-alert state.**

3. Envision and Embody

For the 15- 30 minutes, you will actively enter and inhabit the persona of your Ideal Self.

Ask yourself: What does this ideal person feel like? What internal certainty do they possess? How do they respond to pressure?

Gently introduce the feeling and the conviction of this Ideal Self into your awareness. **Sustain this feeling** as the singular object of your focus. Experience the identity now, knowing that your feeling is your frequency.

4. Practice the Return

Whenever distracting thoughts or doubts about your self-arise, do not engage them.

Immediately use the **"Load the Leaf"** technique to gently release the thought.

Then, gently but firmly return your feeling and focus to the unshakable conviction of your Ideal Self.

C. The Key to Transformation

The power of this discipline lies in the fact that you are not visualizing a future event but choosing a present identity. The sustained feeling of being the Ideal Self creates an internal shift that compels the subconscious mind to reorganize thoughts, emotions, and actions to match your new self-concept

Finding the Core Desire: A Personal Realization

My spiritual advisor and I were talking in his office again and he asked me, **"What do you want?"**

Up to that point in my life, this was a dreaded question. For years, due to what I would term mental abuse as a child, I doubted I could be anything; I was told I would not amount to anything. That had dealt a real blow to my self-esteem, which took a conscious effort to rebuild.

When John D., my advisor, asked me what I wanted, the words that came out of my mouth were simply, "The best person I can be." It was vague, but it was all I could think of. I wasn't even sure what it meant, other than an improved sense of self, and that it might make life better somehow.

John replied, "You want to feel better, right?"

You see, he knew me better than I knew myself, and he had 'hit the nail on the head' with that comment. I immediately replied, "YES!" The idea of **feeling good** hit home, and I knew it could cover lots of ground for me in my life at the time. Of course, feeling good was a foreign concept to me. To that point, I had spent my life escaping and avoiding feeling anything.

But the point I want to make here is that a crucial component to the improved self, and the changing and growing, is to **feel good**. This is not only logically sound, but vital to manifesting anything good and/or positive in anyone's life.

This brings us back to the heart of motivation: the **inner thirst** that drives true change. We can show you the water—the principles and practices for emotional well-being—but you must be willing to drink. For many, like me in the past, the challenge isn't the lack of desire to feel better, but the **fear and guilt that prohibit receiving it**. It is difficult to allow yourself to feel good when you have been conditioned to low self-worth. Therefore, the key is to recognize that emotional well-being is not an all-or-nothing demand. The goal is simply to **allow yourself to feel as much—or as little—goodness as you can handle today.**

I once asked a gentleman who was diligently applying these principles, "How are you?" One day, he replied with a laugh, **"If it gets any better, I'm gonna scream!"** I knew exactly what he meant. Your capacity to receive positive feeling will grow with practice, but you must grant yourself permission to start drinking from the well even if it is only a sip. Start by deliberately doing what you believe is best for you. If you are unsure what that is at the moment, **seek the thoughtful perspective of a trusted person.** However, remember that seeking advice only serves you if you are **willing to truly listen and apply it.**

VII Integrity

The Foundation of Integrity: Wholeness and Truth

The term **integrity** originates from the Latin word integer, meaning whole, complete, or sound. This is the ultimate aspiration of this principle: to live a **whole and integrated life** where your actions, beliefs, and inner truths are in alignment. This profound state of soundness is essential for achieving the cosmic harmony this book describes.

Why is integrity so important? It is the bedrock of inner strength and trust. When you operate from integrity, you free yourself from the draining energy of secrecy and self-deception. It is how one begins to build a life that feels authentic and complete, regardless of external circumstances.

You show integrity by choosing to live in truth. This means:

Being radically **honest** with yourself and others.

Allowing others to see you as you are, without putting on a false front.

Taking **responsibility** for your actions and character.

Following through on your **commitments** to yourself and others.

Admitting mistakes swiftly and without defensiveness, which is exactly what this chapter addresses.

Building integrity is a daily practice anchored in **vulnerability** and improved self-awareness. When you are vulnerable enough to examine your weaknesses (as you did in the inventory) and share them (as you will in the disclosure), you become immune to the fear of exposure. That willingness to be seen completely—strengths and limitations alike—is what makes you whole.

The true golden rule of integrity can serve as your immediate guide for all choices, spoken or unspoken: **"If it is not right, don't do it. If it is not true, don't say it."**

The Act of Self-Disclosure

After taking a fearless and thorough moral inventory, the next crucial commitment is to share your findings. This is the ultimate act of **integrity**, and it's where the hard work of introspection truly begins to pay off. It may feel daunting, but without a follow-up of this kind, the unburdening process remains incomplete, leaving the burden of secrets behind to fester.

The act of sharing your inventory with a trusted person is a form of spiritual and psychological release. For too long, you may have carried the weight of your liabilities and the burden of your past in silence. Confession isn't about being judged or punished; it's about putting your secrets out into the open, where they lose their power over you. By speaking your truth, you free yourself from the isolation that shame and guilt they create. When this self-disclosure is complete, you will experience a profound and absolute shift. The immediate feeling is one of being cleansed and completely unburdened, marking the undeniable start of a fresh consciousness and a new beginning.

The Necessity of Shedding the Burden

a. Pocketing Your Pride: Sharing your weaknesses and shortcomings with another person requires immense humility. Your ego will likely resist this step, telling you that it's a sign of weakness to admit your faults. But the truth is, it takes far more **courage** to be vulnerable than it does to maintain a false front. This process is a direct confrontation with pride, a character trait that often stands in the way of true spiritual progress. I can honestly say that my own false pride nearly killed me. It is this act of humbly revealing your inner world that allows you to gain the integrity and strength that pride could never provide.

b. You're as Sick as Your Secrets: Your secrets are a source of illness in your   life, both mentally and spiritually. They fester in the dark corners of your mind, attracting fear, anxiety, and resentment. They are a continuous drain on your energy and a block to your shining light and connection with those closest to you. By bringing your secrets into the light, you heal the very part of you that has been held captive. Sharing your inventory is a testament to your newfound integrity, the willingness to live in truth, not in the shadows. So, allow the brilliance of your newly cleansed consciousness to shine forth.

Rising Above: The Spiritual Conditioning of the New Self

The moral inventory and the self-disclosure were the processes of unburdening yourself, but rising above is the essential act of ongoing victory. It is the moment you choose to inhabit the new **identity** you have created. Rising above is not about fighting or conquering your old self; it is about withdrawing your energy and focus from the person you were and consciously pouring it into the person you are becoming.

This is a shift in identity. You are no longer identifying with your liabilities; you are identifying with your Ideal Self. Think of this as spiritual conditioning: you are training your mind and spirit to operate at a higher frequency. The process is simple in its design, though not always easy in its execution. This practice involves two key disciplines you must practice daily:

Mindful Awareness: Consciously notice when an old habit or thought pattern arises. Simply observe it without judgment and acknowledge it as a remnant of the past.

Deliberate Action: Choose a new, more constructive action or thought in that moment. The simplicity of this two-step process bellies its power. By consistently making these small choices, you build the spiritual muscle needed to rise above your old self and live in a new, more conscious way. Remember, every effort counts and is recognized as conscious choice for a positive or more constructive thought or behavior.

VIII Maturity and Growth

Introduction: The Law of Rhythm -Flow of Life

As you embark on the path of self-improvement and maturity, it is vital to understand that progress is not linear. This truth is governed by the **Law of Rhythm,** which states: "Everything flows, out and in; everything has its tides; all things rise and fall."

This principle describes the cyclical and rhythmic nature of the universe, assuring you that every aspect of life—including your emotions, energy, success, and character development—swings like a pendulum. You will experience periods of high motivation and progress (the "flow" or "rise") followed by inevitable periods of stagnation or even regression (the "ebb" or "fall"). It's simply the nature of existence, and accepting this reality is another step toward mastery. The key to mastery then, is not to eliminate the downward swing, which is impossible, but to recognize it as a natural, temporary phase. When you are experiencing the "ebb," the Law of Rhythm teaches you to maintain your mental equilibrium. Use your **Intentional Will** to consciously refuse to be swept away by the negative momentum, knowing that the cycle will inevitably swing back toward progress.

Life is difficult to be sure; and growth without pain is growth in vain. When I was told that, I thought to myself, 'Oh gosh, do I have to?'' The answer is a resounding YES for all of us. This difficult work is the very nature of growing up. Maturity is the ability to maintain faith and focus on the positive pole, even when the current rhythm seems to be dragging you backward. Thus, inner growth yields inner strength—the essential strength required for shedding the old self.

1. The Inner Shift: Are you ready to Shed the Old Self

The pivotal question you must answer is whether you are truly ready to embrace this change. After the moral inventory and the act of confession, you'll find yourself standing at a spiritual crossroads. This is where you begin the deliberate process of shedding the old self—the negative habits, character defects, and shortcomings you've identified.

A fair warning: your ego might resist this shift. You may find yourself clinging to some of these things at first, even if they are not constructive. You'll want to 'hang onto' some of the old and familiar thought patterns. But, the whole idea is to exchange old ideas for new ones, bad habits for constructive ones, and scattered consciousness for a more concentrated one. Ultimately, you are striving to form a new ideal from which a new you, and as a result, a new life, will emerge. Your progress in change won't be obvious to you, but it will be to others. Seeing yourself completely objectively is not to be expected. It is much easier for others to make that objective observation.

Cultivating Humility

As you begin to shed your old self, you may encounter this vital distinction. **Humility is an accurate and modest assessment of oneself, recognizing both strengths and limitations without an inflated ego or self-deprecation**. It's a state of mind and a choice that you make. While **humiliation** is an external experience where one's pride or dignity is painfully wounded, often inflicted by others or circumstances. It's something done to you. The difference lies in autonomy. Humility is self-chosen and empowering, while humiliation is imposed and disempowering. By cultivating humility, you free yourself from the fear of being humiliated. It adds to your peace of mind and allows you to learn from mistakes and connect with others authentically.

b) Essential Knowledge (Understanding Brain/Mind-Spirit)

A vital part of personal growth and awakening is gaining foundational knowledge, a staple for expanding conscious insight and strengthening the self. Your brain is the hardware, and you are the one who writes the software—the code it executes. That code is your conscious insight, knowledge, and beliefs you choose to install.

Understanding Your Brain: While complex, understanding your brain's basic functions empowers you. Your thoughts and beliefs shape your reality and understanding how they form allows for intentional change. Emotions are messengers, not masters, and your ability to manage them comes from understanding their origin. The brain's efficiency in creating routines (both good and bad) is the basis of habit formation, and by understanding this, you can intentionally cultivate new positive habits.

The Mind-Spirit Connection: Understand that your mind and spirit are not separate but interconnected. For this book, we define "spirit" as our deepest essence, intuition, source of purpose, or connection to something larger than ourselves. The spiritual aspect complements the mental, offering guidance, resilience, and a sense of meaning that logic alone can't provide. The strengthening of one naturally supports and strengthens the other in the awakening process.

2. The Gradual Bloom: Actionable Steps

Tools for Continuous Unfolding

(Observation, Resources, Journaling)

This isn't a course of study with a fixed endpoint; it is a dynamic journey of continuous discovery and life mastery. The ultimate goal of this work is realizing and recognizing your inner divinity. This profound recognition is achieved through a committed inner process: undertaking a personal inventory, making truthful self-disclosure, and maintaining a sincere, continual desire to change. The objective here isn't to become an expert or a spiritual authority; it is to gain actionable insight for profound personal application and sustained spiritual growth. And there is no spiritual growth unless you wholly immerse yourself in this undertaking—from admitting character flaws and recognizing your assets to achieving self-realization and ultimately being of service to others (Chapter XI). The development of Conscious Awareness serves as the arrow of right direction, guiding your way through this continuous unfolding.

Conscious Observation: As we have been emphasizing, pay strict attention to YOUR OWN thoughts, feelings, and reactions. You are your only patient. While you should never ignore others, remember that your focus is on self-treatment and self-correction. You are responsible only for your own inner world, and you must resist the temptation to manage theirs.

Additional Resources: This book is mainly an overview, a starter kit so to speak. Look for introductory books on neuroscience for personal growth, mindfulness guides, or reputable online articles that help you understand the basics of your inner world.

Reflection and Journaling: These practices help integrate new understandings and make your journey a continuous unfolding. Many people incorporate it into their daily lives.

The Patient's Perspective: "I Am My Only Patient"

Remembering this helps you keep perspective: you cannot change anyone else. However, you retain absolute authority to change your own thoughts and actions.

But here is the key commitment: *do you genuinely want to?* If the answer is yes, then you must change the way you think by training your mind daily and strengthening the thoughts that are in line with the life you want to live.

Understand that this change is not an overnight matter, nor is the goal simply about "getting good." The true goals are the development of **conscious awareness** by which you may **recognize your inner divinity**. The housecleaning process and continued effort to sustain your new identity are designed to clear away the debris that that has clouded your ability to have these realizations. These goals are attained through the **spiritual path,** a path of slow, patient, and steady improvement.

Say the affirmation: I am becoming the ideal me. The operative word is **becoming**—you are always evolving into something. You must start contemplating what that ideal is because YOU get to decide!

The Window of Opportunity

The most hopeful truth revealed by modern behavioral science is that there is a definitive neurological gap—a pause—between the impulse of the old self (the urge to react) and the actual performance of the action. This pause is the moment your Intentional Will is most powerful. By inserting Mindful Awareness into this gap, you seize control of that fleeting space and prevent the automatic reaction.

It is within this divine pause that you shift from being a reactor to being a conscious creator of your reality, proving that old habits have no permanent authority over you. Beginning to feel the freedom yet?

IX Forgiveness

Relationships Define Us

You are important to at least one person who cares about you, even if you are not aware of it. The old and popular phrase, **"no one is an island,"** is true because your very existence is validated through your relations with other people.

Consider the simple connections that define your day: the local mail carrier is YOUR mailperson, and though you may or may not converse, you still think of them, and they think of you. The store clerk knows you for your patronage, even if you only speak at checkout. Other drivers offer a wave of thanks; you return the gesture when they allow you to proceed down the road. These are relations and connections.

Furthermore, you are not simply your job title; you are an employee to someone, a connection that is anything but superficial. Or you may be the boss, and how you relate to those who work for you is an indelible part of who you are. The waiter is YOUR waiter, and that is a relationship. **You are who you are only as your relationships are.**

It may come as a surprise, but relationships don't end. Of course they can change for better or worse, grow, evolve, or dissipate. But they do not end. Even if you haven't spoken to someone for a long time, the connection still exists, albeit in a different form. Since the whole world is connected, you are connected in some form to everybody. Try as you might to distance yourself from the world "out there," you are always connected to humanity, if only mentally. This truth is a deeply comforting and even an exciting discovery when you recognize it.

1. The Key to Healing

Your very existence is tied to your relationships with others; but what happens when those connections are strained or broken? A damaged relationship reflects a dispute, and every dispute has two sides. It is your responsibility to recognize how you contributed to the issue—because that is the only part of the problem you can truly control.

Healing is possible through the power of thought, and **forgiveness** is the key to repairing your inner world. When you forgive another, you **heal yourself.** The same is true when you admit a mistake and apologize; it is a critical part of the healing process. Even if the other person rejects your worthy attempt, you are healed simply by the act of offering it.

Forgiveness vs. Reconciliation

Remember, you are your only patient. **Self-healing must be your first concern.**

Forgiveness is a **unilateral act**; it is something you do for yourself to release the poison of resentment. It is the acceptance of what happened and the release of your attachment to the offense.

Reconciliation is a **bilateral act;** it requires two people and may or may not happen.

This is not to say you should disregard others, but rather that you must take care of yourself first. You cannot be of much use to anyone if you are damaged or ill. So, get well even if for no reason other than for yourself, but especially for yourself! Healing takes time—give it plenty of time. The relationship may not heal, but **you WILL heal if you forgive.**

2. Karma: The Healing Power of Your Actions

Karma concerns itself with the ethical and spiritual domain. It can be understood as the spiritual law of cause and effect in action. It specifically applies to your thoughts, words and deeds and your intension behind them. It is your actions and intentions, whether positive or negative, that have consequences for yourself. For example, by forgiving, you are planting a seed of peace that will ultimately bear fruit in your own life. So your current experiences are the effects of past causes (actions and intentions). Karma means it is inevitable that What goes around comes around.

Kindness, Care, and Consideration Pay Dividends

The act of forgiving, making amends, and living with integrity is a practice in kindness, care, and consideration. These virtues are not just for the benefit of others; they also pay great dividends to your inner world.

When you extend kindness, you immediately raise your own vibrational frequency.

When you give care, you activate a sense of purpose and fulfillment within you.

When you are considerate of others, you align yourself to attract that same consideration.

These are the guaranteed dividends of living a conscious and connected life.

Live and Let Live

Take this phrase literally; you live your life and let the other person live theirs. This idea of "live and let live" is a powerful tool for maintaining your own inner peace and is a direct route to freedom. By granting others the freedom to be themselves—just as you seek the freedom to be yourself—you release yourself from a heavy mental burden. It also doubles as a form of forgiveness in action. It is a quiet way of saying, "I choose my own peace over the need to be right." One time while discussing a relationship problem with my old friend, he asked me, "Do you want to be right, or do you want to be happy?" That gave me pause and I had to honestly consider those alternatives. I'll admit, there were times I so wanted to be right. But in the end, what I really wanted was peace of mind and happiness. When you apply this principle, you will discover it's not just a saying but a definite and powerful function for your own peace of mind.

So when you accept that you cannot control the actions or thoughts of others, you let go of judgment and the desire to impose your will on them. I found it to be liberating and you will too.

3. Daily Persistence: The Practice of Ongoing Vigilance

Spiritual growth and healing is a daily process requiring persistence. It is about growing in understanding and conscious awareness. This continuous practice requires you to stay alert to your own shortcomings, consistently noticing where your thinking or actions have had a negative impact on someone else, and then making the necessary amends to rectify the wrong. The more you do this, the more natural it will become. But the key is constant vigilance.

Continue to Watch Yourself: You are your only patient. Since your first responsibility is to yourself, it requires you to keep watch. Make a daily practice of paying strict attention to your thoughts, feelings, and actions. When resentment or anger forms, use the healing power of forgiveness to diffuse it.

Admit Wrongs Promptly: Do not let a mistake fester. If you have caused harm to another, make amends as soon as you are aware of it. This simple act of integrity prevents resentment from growing and helps you live in harmony with the cosmos.

Forgiveness is **freedom** from the heavy burden of resentments, hurtful attitudes, and fears. It empowers you to live a life of peace, connection, and enduring joy. Some relationships may not heal, but you will heal when you forgive.

X Illumined Mind

Mastering the Cosmic Flow

The goal of this entire journey is to grow spiritually and ultimately achieve the dual aims of **sustaining a vibrant, continuous state of conscious awareness** and subsequently **recognizing your inherent inner divinity**. While the previous chapters provided the necessary foundation through mental control disciplines, affirmations, and deliberate practice, the true aim of this continuous unfolding is to transcend mere effort and establish **enlightenment**—an effortless, intuitive 'knowing' of your true nature.

The Illumined Mind is not simply about powerful thought, but about realizing your direct, conscious connection to the Source of all energy. This profound connection is a deeply personal experience—there is no right or wrong way to achieve it. The most important thing is to be open to its possibility and allow yourself to be guided by your intuition. When this connection is established, you immediately feel more inspired, more motivated, and more hopeful, leading to a profound sense of connection with everything.

This chapter introduces five practical and immediate daily practices designed to accelerate your conscious awakening and cultivate this Illumined Mind.

The journey toward conscious living, or realizing "cosmic harmony," begins with understanding the most fundamental force of existence: **Prana.** This Sanskrit term is far more profound than its usual translation of 'breath.' Prana is the **universal life force energy** that animates all existence—from the vast cosmos to every living cell within. It is the subtle, unseen engine of vitality, the link between the physical body, the mind, and the spirit. Without it, life simply cannot exist.

In yogic and Ayurvedic traditions, Prana is the invisible thread that connects body, mind, and spirit. While often associated with the air you breathe, Prana is the subtle energy within the air, absorbed not only through the breath, but also from food, water, sunlight, and even sensory experiences. This energy flows through thousands of subtle channels called nadis and collects in energy centers known as chakras. The quality and volume of Prana moving through these channels determine your overall health, mental clarity, and spiritual awareness. When Prana is abundant and flowing freely, you feel energized, focused, and emotionally balanced.

1. The Practice of Presence and Regulation

The most accessible and immediate manifestation of Prana in the human body is the breath. This is where the profound practice begins: Your breath is the simplest path to presence because it is the direct link between the body and the conscious mind. **Stop, take a deep breath, exhale slowly, and sincerely say "Thank you."**

This simple act marks the beginning of understanding that life is a precious gift and that breath is the essential link between the mind and body. This is the first action toward harmonizing with the cosmos and forming a positive mindset to begin your day.

The ancient science developed to control and direct this life force is called Pranayama. Composed of two roots—Prana (life force) and Ayama (extension or expansion)—**Pranayama** is the systematic practice of controlling and extending the breath to harness, store, and manipulate the flow of Prana within the body. It is one of the most powerful tools employed by **the Intentional Will.** Here is how the practice of Pranayama helps to regulate this vital energy:

Directing Energy: By bringing conscious awareness to the movement of your breath, you're not just moving air; you're actively directing the flow of Prana within your body. This intentional direction can help to energize certain areas, calm others, and ultimately bring a sense of balance.

Calming the Mind: The mind and breath are intimately connected. Regulating the breath (through Pranayama) directly influences the nervous system, shifting it from a "fight or flight" (sympathetic) state to a "rest and digest" (parasympathetic) state, naturally calming the mind.

Enhancing Awareness: Sustained attention on the breath acts as an anchor, bringing you into the present moment and fostering conscious awareness. It's like turning up the volume on your internal experience.

Purification and Vitality: Conscious breathing practices are believed to purify the subtle energy channels (nadis) and energy centers (chakras), allowing Prana to flow more freely. This enhanced flow leads to increased vitality, improved physical health, and greater mental clarity.

Recommended Further Reading For individuals both familiar and new to the concepts of Prana and breathing exercises, here are highly regarded options to deepen your practice and understanding:

Essential Pranayama: Breathing Techniques for Balance, Healing, and Peace by Gerry Givens: This book is widely regarded for anyone interested in breathwork. It bridges the gap between ancient yogic traditions and modern scientific understanding, providing a holistic perspective on its effects.

Light on Pranayama: The Yogic Art of Breathing by B.K.S. Iyengar: This is a foundational text for anyone serious about Pranayama. It offers meticulous instructions on various breathing techniques with an ideal methodical and disciplined approach.

Breath: The New Science of a Lost Art by James Nestor: This book offers a fascinating, scientifically backed exploration of breathing, delving into its profound physiological and psychological impacts, making it an engaging and motivating read from a modern perspective.

Prana and Pranayama by Swami Niranjanananda Saraswati: An extremely comprehensive text from the Bihar School of Yoga. This work is ideal for serious students and teachers, as it offers a deep dive into both the theoretical philosophy and the practical application of advanced techniques.

The Yoga Sutras of Patanjali (Various Translators): While not exclusively about breath, this classical foundational text places Pranayama into its complete philosophical context, providing the ancient framework for why breath control is critical to calming the fluctuations of the mind.

The Discipline of the Flow (Leaves on a Stream)

To experience an illumined mind, you must master the art of **mental detachment**—observing thoughts without engaging them. When adverse or stressful thoughts arise during your practices, don't fight them; just release them to the flow of Universal Energy.

A beautiful method for this is the **"Leaves on a Stream"** technique:

Visualize the Scene: Close your eyes and vividly imagine a river flowing gently and steadily before you. Notice the smooth current and the banks of the stream.

Observe the Flow: Imagine any number or size of leaves floating slowly by on the surface of the water.

Place the Thought: When a thought, worry, or adverse condition arises— be it worry, doubt, fear, or a resentment—mentally place that thought, as a word or an image, directly onto one of the passing leaves.

Release and Repeat: Watch the leaf, carrying the thought, floating downstream until it vanishes around the bend. You simply allow it to leave you. Now return your focus to the gentle flow and wait for the next leaf. This discipline teaches your conscious mind that thoughts are not commands; they are simply objects that can be observed and released just like that.

2. Prayer

"Therefore I tell you, whatever you ask for in prayer,

believe that you have received it, and it will be yours" Mark 11:24

Consider the word used to signify the end of a prayer: Amen, which essentially means, so be it. When you say "Amen" after a prayer, you are saying, "I affirm this is true," or "May this be fulfilled." Prayer is one of the most powerful tools for maintaining your connection to the Divine Power or God. It's not about begging for things you want; it's about aligning your mind with a higher power and expressing gratitude for the spiritual riches you already possess. The renowned author Napoleon Hill captured this perfectly:

Divine providence I ask not for more riches, but more wisdom with which to make wiser use of the riches you gave me at birth, consisting in the power to control and direct my own mind to whatever ends I desire. — **Napoleon Hill**

Another prayer that holds a special place in my heart—one used to address impulsive reactions—comes from an unknown source:

THE SPACE BETWEEN- May I have the grace to find the space between my impulse and my action. Let flow a cooling breeze when I would respond with heat. Interrupt fierceness with gentle peace and help me to accept the moment which allows judgment to become discernment and to defer to silence when my tongue would rush to attack or defend. — **Unknown**

This prayer is a powerful guide because it directly addresses the unhealthy impulse to react defensively or aggressively. It asks for the necessary grace to find the pause—the moment of choice—**remember the gap**—which is crucial for maintaining peace of mind and a cheerful outlook.

3. Experience Nature

Another way of nurturing your growth and connection to God is to spend time in nature. This helps you to connect with divinity and experience the **oneness of all things.** Whether it's a walk in the park, a hike in the mountains, or simply sitting in your backyard, experiencing nature helps you attune to the rhythm of life outside of your own thoughts and anxieties. You see, the idea is to take the focus off of yourself for a time and put it on something greater than yourself. So in this way nature is a powerful teacher. It shows us that everything has a purpose and a place in the larger, interconnected whole. You can gain a perspective that can quiet the ego and foster a deeper sense of peace.

4. Recognize Beauty

Illumination is not just about what you do, but also about what you are able to perceive. A conscious practice of awakening involves a deliberate effort to **recognize beauty** in your daily life. This isn't about looking for grand, sweeping vistas; it's about finding beauty in the small, seemingly insignificant details that are all around you.

A single flower growing through a crack in the pavement, the intricate pattern of a spider's web, the way the sunlight hits a window—these are all moments of universal beauty. By consciously seeking out these moments, you train your mind to look for the good in the world, shifting your perspective from one of lack to one of **abundance**.

The practice extends beyond nature to include human connection. For instance, in a previous job driving local travelers to the airport, I started noticing the exchanges between people arriving or departing and their loved ones. Witnessing such profound humanity elevated my spirit and deepened my awareness of the interconnected world and all the beauty to be found within it.

5. Enrich Yourself Through Art and Literature

Finally, art and literature are powerful conduits for spiritual and emotional growth. When you engage with great works or meaningful literature, you enrich your mind and spirit in a way that transcends the ordinary. Consider the art museum, where you experience the immense creative genius of renowned figures. Take some time and learn to appreciate it.

The same is true of music. It can evoke feelings beyond words, and a powerful story can give you a new perspective on human nature. These experiences open your mind to different ways of thinking and feeling, which is key to conscious awakening. By intentionally seeking out art and literature, you give your mind and spirit a chance to expand beyond their usual boundaries, allowing for greater empathy, insight, and understanding. This intentionality, the conscious choice to seek illumination every single day—is the ultimate discipline of an awakened mind.

Unifying Science and Spiritual Energy

When we look beyond the subjective self and ask what the universe is made of, we quickly move past solid matter and into **energy and information**—the realm of quantum physics. At the smallest level (quantum mechanics), matter is not solid; it is vibrating fields of energy and information. The most fundamental "what is" then is a dynamic interconnected field of energy.

While Albert Einstein's famous equation, $E=mc^2$ (Special Relativity, 1905), established the equivalence between mass and energy—telling us they were two faces of the same coin—it did not however, describe the coin's internal nature. That deeper understanding is based on **Quantum Field Theory,** which describes this "dynamic interconnected field of energy and information" as the coin's substructure and core essence. This scientific explanation then is grounding for the Hermetic Law of **Mentalism**, the ultimate reality, stating that all is mind.

It is within this single, conscious reality that all laws operate, chief among them the Law of Flow and Return, or **Energetic Reciprocity**.

In the spiritual and personal development context, the term we call **Energetic Reciprocity** is closely tied to the Law of Karma and the Law of Attraction. It posits that the universe operates on a two-way flow of energy where the quality and intent of the energy you send out *must be returned to you.* The concept stresses the importance of **balanced giving and receiving**. An imbalance—either giving too much and exhausting yourself or taking too much and creating a spiritual deficit—is believed to lead to stagnation or negative outcomes. For example: If you approach your work or relationships with a loving, generous, and cheerful outlook, the principle suggests that the energy you receive back (e.g., in the form of cooperation, fulfillment or opportunity) will reflect that same positive output.

This guaranteed return is not due to a cosmic bookkeeper, but to the nature of the reality in which the transaction occurs. **Universal Mind IS** the source, the single, conscious substance we call **Spiritual Energy**. The ancient wisdom, "what goes around comes around" is literally true and finds its most profound expression in **Energetic Reciprocity**, a principle asserting that all existence is governed by a dynamic, continuous flow of energy that operates within the **Unified Field**. In short, the kind of energy you give is the kind you receive.

While Energetic Reciprocity functions under the Universal Law of Cause and Effect and shares ground with the spiritual Law of Karma, it is not merely a passive accounting system. The key difference is intentionality. It is the active *discipline of the present moment*, empowering you to consciously align your output (giving) to shape your inevitable input (receiving), rather than simply waiting for the consequences of past actions. *Your power over circumstances is exercised not by controlling external events, but by consciously choosing the quality of your inner state, which then dictates the energy you radiate into the Unified Field.*

Think of the Unified Field as being the **ocean** upon which all action takes place. **Energetic Reciprocity** (or Universal Balance/Giving and Receiving) is one of the rules or laws that dictates how energy flows and interacts within the ocean. It can be thought of as the mechanism, or, the action of the tides, so to speak. It's literally the rule governing how the ocean moves and returns reciprocity in dynamic action. It is the cause and effect in the realm of giving and receiving.

The Mechanism of Flow: Energetic Reciprocity vs. Related Laws

Concept	Core Function	Primary Focus
1. Cause and Effect (The Universal Law)	The most fundamental, **impersonal** law. Every action creates a corresponding reaction.	**Mechanism.** Describes *how* the universe operates without judging intent or quality.
2. Karma (The Spiritual Law)	The moral application of Cause and Effect. Actions (physical, mental, verbal) create a stored spiritual imprint that will return to the actor, often across lifetimes.	**Accountability and Consequence.** Focus on the accumulated *debt or merit* of past actions and their ultimate return. It is often passive, dealing with fate.
3. Energetic Reciprocity (The Conscious Discipline)	The immediate, intentional flow of energy (giving and receiving). The **quality and intent** of energy put out returns in kind, often quickly.	**Active Co-creation.** Focus on the *present-moment choice* of intent and alignment, emphasizing flow rather than debt or obligation. It's an active choice.

This law posits that every thought, emotion, and action we initiate is a form of energetic currency—a seed planted in the cosmos. Our external reality, therefore, is not dictated by luck or random chance, but represents the inevitable harvest of the quality of energy we have consistently sown. The key to understanding Energetic Reciprocity is to recognize that we are not merely passive participants in life, but active co-creators who directly shape our world by the intention and consciousness we radiate within a spiritual, metaphysical, and social context.

The reason these spiritual laws hold true is rooted in the structure of existence itself. Remember that reality operates on the two-level model: the Ultimate Reality (the source) is boundless, and your personal experience takes place in the limiting, transactional world of Empirical Reality (the result). Our work, therefore, is always to bring the freedom of the Ultimate Truth into the forefront of individual experience.

XI Love and Service

The Ultimate Realization:

Love is Divine Oneness

Physicists and philosophers often use the term **'Unified Field'** when referring to the single, fundamental continuum or source from which all forces and matter arise. It is static reality or the substance of the universe. We have recognized this field as the non-dual, conscious substance of Mentalism that connects all things.

The Inherent Nature of this truth is that because **Spiritual Energy** is the only existing substance, it acts as the common denominator from which all phenomena (you, me, stars, energy) flow. This unified connectivity is known as **Divine Oneness**. It is the absolute truth that all things are literally made of the same intelligence and are connected at the source.

Therefore, since the **Universal Mind** (or Source) is everything, and everything within it is connected, we are not merely separate beings existing outside of or even 'near' the Divine. No, not at all! I, you, we, and they are all expressions of the same source and are fundamentally one with each other. This is the ultimate realization of **Divine Oneness**. Every one of us may only be a drop in an ocean but, we are still the ocean.

You are a Channel of Expression: Give It Away to Keep It

It follows then that there is a spiritual axiom that says you must give it away to keep it. The secret to power and success doesn't depend on what you accumulate, but on unselfishness and your ability to be of service. This isn't about sacrifice; it's about abundance. What you give, you receive. As "Tree Farm George" wisely put it, "Success is not measured by what you can get, it's measured by what you can give." Spiritual growth is contingent on thoughts toward others of good health, inspiration, encouragement, or help of any kind.

This is the way to keep the channel open, allowing kindness, care, and consideration to flow your way as well.

The important thing is to give something from the heart, and without expectation of being reciprocated. Intention is key, in that the quality of what you receive is believed to be directly proportionate to the intention behind your giving. In other words, giving joyfully, unconditionally and from the heart is seen as more powerful than giving grudgingly or with a hidden expectation.

But what about the person who thinks they have nothing to offer? What about a poor person who, in the monetary sense, has little or nothing to give? They will be thinking, I must have enough for myself and/ or my family! I will add, and rightly so. It is entirely reasonable and understandable to think that way.

So we ask, how does one begin to develop a mindset of abundance in the first place if they have hitherto only known poverty, loss and lack? We start by stating that limit and lack thoughts are 'rocky soil,' not particularly good for planting the seeds you wish to grow. Abundance mindset on the other hand is soft fertile soil; it is the perfect ground for planting and reaping a harvest.

With this in mind, giving is about watering the soil. A non-monetary focus is appropriate and logical. Obviously, one cannot give something they do not have. But here is the vital point, you must only focus on what you DO HAVE-that is the whole idea. So in this sense, the only cost is a moment of conscious effort. The bottom line is this: The spiritual law is not a credit-debit system; it is an actual law of nature.

I will elaborate. A farmer sows seeds in the spring. Is the farmer giving without expectation? No, the farmer absolutely expects a harvest. This expectation is a rational part of the process.

Is the farmer selfish? No. The farmer focuses all their energy on the quality of the action, tilling the soil, watering, and protecting the seed. They don't dig up the seed every day to check on it, nor do they resent the earth for not instantly producing a carrot.

On the other hand, if the farmers approach were selfish, it would be like giving a seed and staring at the ground, demanding, "Where is my return?" Pretty absurd right? To be aligned then, is giving a seed and focusing on the integrity of the soil and the process, knowing that harvest is a certainty. But always remember that the timing and form are not dictated by the giver.

Therefore, the act of aligning yourself with the process—focusing your intent on the quality of the giving (tilling the soil) rather than demanding the result—transforms harvest from a hope into a certainty.

The axiom is not just about material things as we have noted.

The most valuable gifts are often considered non-material, such as:

- **Appreciation and compliments**

- **Undivided attention**

- **A simple genuine smile or silent blessing.**

- **Gentle and respectful affection**

Transaction vs. Flow

It is a common philosophical obstacle people encounter when first learning about the law of reciprocity (or Sowing and Reaping) i.e., if the primary motivation for giving is to get something back, the action is, by definition, transactional and ultimately selfish. The key to clearing this mental block lies in understanding the difference between a Transaction and universal flow.

Selfishness arises when we confuse the 'worldly social rule of reciprocity (which is transactional) with the Spiritual Law of Reciprocity (which is about energetic alignment). The following chart explains:

Concept	The transactional mindset (Selfish)	The spiritual flow mindset (Non-Attached)
Focus	The return: *"I hope this person notices, so they owe me a favor."*	The Action: *"I choose to express kindness/abundance now."*
Source of Return	Certain person/entity: Expecting the return to come directly from the person you helped, or you track the "debt."	The Universe/Life: Trusting the return will come from *any* source, in the best form, and at the right time.
Result	Disappointment & Resentment: If the person doesn't pay you back, you feel cheated; the flow stops.	Peace & Abundance: The joy is in the giving; the return is a bonus and a sign of alignment.

What Fuels Abundance? The Role of Intentional Giving

You fuel abundance by moving your intention away from the result and focus entirely on the present moment and quality of the gift and giving without attachment.

Your focus should be on identity; instead of asking, "What will I get for doing this?" ask, "What kind of person am I choosing to be right now?" If you choose sincerity, kindness, and generosity, then sincerity, kindness, and abundance are what you are radiating into your life. The return is simply the universe reflecting your chosen state of being. The act of giving is simply an expression of your inner abundance, not a mechanism to fill your inner lack.

The Gift of Joy

The highest form of giving is the one where the act of giving itself is the reward. When you give a sincere compliment, or you genuinely help someone, the immediate, non-selfish return is the internal feeling of joy and connection that sparks within you. This immediate feeling is the first return of the Law of Reciprocity. You have already received payment, which allows you to release the expectation of a future, material one.

In summary, "The Spiritual Law of Reciprocity" is not about transactional debt. It's about alignment. We don't give to get; we give because we are choosing to be the energy of abundance. We trust the law because it's a mechanism of the universe, like gravity. The intention is not to collect a debt, but to express our true nature and keep the universal flow of energy moving. You intentionally shift the focus from a selfish "what's in it for me?" to an aligned "I choose to be a source of good, because I am one with the source."

This conscious and deliberate choice is the **application of Love**. People naturally respond to Love; it truly is the force that keeps the world turning. **Love is not just a feeling; it is the active principle and the most powerful energy in existence.** It has the capacity to heal, transform, and bring people together. When you choose to Love, you align yourself with the **Law of Divine Oneness.** This is the foundational truth of spiritual growth: the more you give, the more you receive in return.

Abundance is not a stagnant pool but a dynamic exchange—a continuous flow. For those new to this mindset, giving can seem difficult, but the truth is, you always possess something valuable to offer. Furthermore, the ability to receive graciously is just as vital as the ability to give. Below is a guide to help you initiate this flow, demonstrating how even small, non-material gifts translate into profound spiritual payoffs.

The Daily Practices of Giving Chart

Exchange (The Giving)	Flow of Action (The Practice)	Benefit (The Receiving)
Emotional / Non-Material	**Silent Wish / Blessing:** Spend a moment each day sending a thoughtful, positive outcome (good health, happiness, prosperity) to someone you know or a stranger.	**Increased Self-Worth & Inner Peace:** You cultivate inner peace by having positive intent. Your self-worth increases as you realize you are one with the source.
Time / Service	**Undivided Attention:** When speaking with someone, dedicate your full, non-judgmental attention without checking your phone or planning your response.	**Improved, Deeper Connections & New Opportunities:** You create trust and connection. Your focus expands your awareness, leading to unexpected insights and breakthroughs.
Mindfulness / Active Presence	**Acknowledgment:** Consciously acknowledge and affirm the divine spark in others by offering a **genuine smile**, a heartfelt "hello," or a nod. This intentional act prevents the negative impact of omission and strengthens your connection.	**Renewed Sense of Purpose & Appreciation:** You break the habit of taking things for granted. Gratitude expands your present moment experience of abundance. A little gratitude goes a long way.
Material / Financial	**Intentional Tithing/Donation:** Give a small amount of money (even pennies) or a physical item with the conscious understanding that you are affirming your faith in the source of your supply.	**Prosperity & Confidence in the Source:** You destroy the fear of lack. Your confidence in the resource flow (Spiritual Energy) increases, leading to greater prosperity.

The Necessity of Receiving

It is clear that we must possess something before we can give it. John D. wisely said, "You need an abundance of Love before you can give Love." He elaborated: "When you have enough for yourself and some left over—that's an abundance of it." This realization makes learning to receive graciously a vital part of the flow. It does not matter which end of the spectrum you start from; your work is to learn to accept caring, understanding, acceptance, and affection. I know this from firsthand experience. I was one of those people who cringed when someone got close. I was leery of letting anyone being too close for fear of being touched or showing care, often out of a deep discomfort with my own feelings. Yet, the sooner you allow yourself to be "okay" with a hug or a gentle loving touch, the sooner you'll find yourself naturally passing on that affection.

The Ultimate Expression

Love is the active principle and the most powerful energy in existence. When you consciously choose to Love, you align yourself with the Law of Divine Oneness. This is the foundational truth of spiritual growth: the more you give, the more you receive in return. John D.'s life, and the example of **John 13:34–35** that he lived—**"A new commandment I give to you, that you love one another: just as I have loved you, you also are to love one another"**—is a testament to this truth.

At its deepest level, Love is best expressed through four essential values. And again, I attribute them to John D.

The Four Values of Love

These four values are not intangibles or mere feelings, but conscious action that serve as the ultimate expression of your awakened life:

1. Caring with Concern

To care for someone is to hold their well-being in your thoughts and actions. It's an empathetic connection that goes beyond a superficial exchange. Caring with concern means this person is important enough to be actively listening to them. And when you do, you are being present in their moments of joy and sorrow and offering support without expectation of anything in return.

It's a genuine investment in the happiness of others. When you show authentic concern, you're not just offering a kind gesture; you're acknowledging the shared humanity between you and another person, reaffirming your spiritual connection. People need to know that someone cares.

2. Understanding with Patience

You have no doubt heard the saying, patience is a virtue. It is because understanding with patience is the ability to see others as they are, flaws and all, without judgment. We are all on our own unique paths, and no individual person is perfect.

So understanding with patience means recognizing that people's actions often stem from their own struggles and pain. Instead of reacting with anger or frustration, you can respond with a compassionate heart. This practice is a direct expression of the growth you've cultivated throughout this book, allowing you to choose a peaceful response over an impulsive reaction. Patience isn't about waiting; it's about holding space for others to be human and yes, allowing time for them to understand themselves better. We all need this at some point.

3. Acceptance with Trust

Acceptance with Trust is the practice of letting go of the need to change people or situations. It's an act of surrender rooted in the truth of the **Two-Level Model:** everyone is on their own unique journey. Remember, beneath the surface of all our separate waves and ripples, we are all the same ocean. It's not that we're all in the same boat—there is no boat; we are the vast, vaster than all the oceans.

You accept people for who they are and still hold them in a place of trust, believing in their inherent goodness and capacity for growth. It is this form of love that frees you from resentment and the desire to control. By trusting in the ultimate efficacy of Universal Law (that everyone is subject to their own cause and effect), you find freedom in your own alignment. This doesn't mean you should allow others to harm you; true acceptance means releasing the desire to control them while fiercely honoring your own boundaries.

4. Affection with Respect

This final value is the outward expression of the first three. Affection with respect is the conscious practice of showing warmth and kindness to everyone you encounter. This can be a gentle touch or as simple as a genuine smile, a kind word, or a heartfelt thank you. It's a way of honoring the divine spark within every person. When you treat others with respect and high regard, you are affirming their value and, in doing so, are strengthening your own. This value is a daily reminder that love is an action, not just a feeling.

Recommended Further Reading on Love:

These books offer deeper philosophical practical perspectives on cultivating love as a conscious skill, reinforcing its role as the ultimate principle of the awakened life:

<u>The Art of Loving</u> by Erich Fromm: This foundational classic explores love not as a feeling but as an **art** requiring knowledge, discipline, and effort. It perfectly supports the idea that love is an **active practice** you must cultivate daily.

<u>All About Love: New Visions</u> by bell hooks: A powerful, contemporary book that defines love as "the will to extend oneself for the purpose of nurturing one's own or another's spiritual growth."

<u>A Course in Miracles</u> (Foundation for Inner Peace): Its core spiritual framework centers on the idea that the practice of **forgiveness** is the key to removing the obstacles (fear) that block the awareness of love's presence.

Epilogue: The Conscious Creator

In closing, this journey has been a return to the self. You first learned about conscious-awareness and recognizing your true self. Then you crossed the boundaries of a conditioned mind to being awakened to a conscious mind. The world is not at the command of an invisible hand, but a conscious one: yours. You have discovered that a thinking mind seeks the "why," an inner mind houses the silent servant of the will, and an empowered mind is your true force. You've learned to be a guardian at the gate of your own consciousness, protecting your peace through forgiveness and strengthening your spirit through service. You now understand that you are not separate from the world but are a walking, talking expression of a single, unifying force.

The work is not complete, but it is no longer a mystery. The destination is not an endpoint but a **continuous state of conscious experience**. Your awakening to conscious living has come full circle, and you are no longer the Nowhere Man, but the **conscious creator** of your own experience. You now wield the **Law of Energetic Reciprocity**, and the universe will respond in kind to your shining light.

"...And in the end, the love you take Is equal to the love you make."

The Beatles, The End

Namaste

www.ingramcontent.com/pod-product-compliance
Lightning Source LLC
Chambersburg PA
CBHW020605160726
47991CB00002B/884